500 ART QUILTS

AN INSPIRING COLLECTION OF CONTEMPORARY WORK

LARK BOOKS

A Division of Sterling Publishing Co., Inc.
New York / London

SENIOR EDITOR
Ray Hemachandra

EDITOR
Julie Hale

ART DIRECTOR
Kay Holmes Stafford

COVER DESIGNER
Celia Naranjo

FRONT COVER
Nancy Murty
Love, Honor, and Cherish, 2004

BACK COVER
Linda Gass
South Bay, 2006

SPINE
Wendy Butler Berns
Reflections of God's Skin, 2004

FRONT FLAP
Linda Barlow
One Day I'll Fly Away with the Birds and the Fishes, 2003

BACK FLAP
Judy Coates Perez
Moon Garden, 2008

OPPOSITE
Pat Kumicich
We're All the Same—Just Different, 2006

TITLE PAGE
Gwyned Trefethen
Botswana Bounty, 2008

Library of Congress Cataloging-in-Publication Data

500 art quilts : an inspiring collection of contemporary work / senior editor, Ray Hemachandra.
    p. cm.
  Includes index.
  ISBN 978-1-60059-058-0 (pb-pbk. with flaps : alk. paper)
  1. Art quilts--History--21st century. I. Hemachandra, Ray. II. Title: Five hundred art quilts.

  NK9110.5.A14 2010
  746.46--dc22

                                    2009023172

10 9 8 7 6 5 4 3 2

Published by Lark Books, A Division of
Sterling Publishing Co., Inc.
387 Park Avenue South, New York, NY 10016

Text © 2010, Lark Books, A Division of Sterling Publishing Co., Inc.
Photography © 2010, Artist/Photographer

Distributed in Canada by Sterling Publishing,
c/o Canadian Manda Group, 165 Dufferin Street
Toronto, Ontario, Canada M6K 3H6

Distributed in the United Kingdom by GMC Distribution Services,
Castle Place, 166 High Street, Lewes, East Sussex, England BN7 1XU

Distributed in Australia by Capricorn Link (Australia) Pty Ltd.,
P.O. Box 704, Windsor, NSW 2756 Australia

If you have questions or comments about this book, please contact:
Lark Books
67 Broadway,
Asheville, NC 28801
828-253-0467

Manufactured in China

ISBN 13: 978-1-60059-058-0

For information about custom editions, special sales, and premium and corporate purchases, please
contact the Sterling Special Sales Department at 800-805-5489 or specialsales@sterlingpub.com

For information about desk and examination copies available to college and university
professors, requests must be submitted to academic@larkbooks.com. Our complete policy
can be found at www.larkbooks.com.

Contents

Introduction by Karey Patterson Bresenhan, Juror   6

The Quilts   8

About the Juror   428

Acknowledgments   428

Contributing Artists   429

Introduction

Although it happened almost 30 years ago, I can still recall the time I saw my first art quilt. I was attending the 1982 International Quilt Festival in Houston, Texas, and an art quilt—Katie Pasquini Masopust's *Threshold of a Dream*—turned out to be the surprise winner of the festival's Best of Show award. The judge that year was Jinny Beyer, the acknowledged queen of old-fashioned quilt making. The idea that Jinny, a devotee of "slow quilts" and handwork, would select an abstract wall piece over the gorgeous traditional creations entered in the show was shocking. Her choice turned the quilt world upside down.

Quilts created as art, destined from their inception to be displayed on walls, began to be noticed and acknowledged during the last quarter of the twentieth century. These art pieces are made with needle and thread instead of paint and brushes, but their creators' kinship to the painters of the past is as strong as their connection to women who hand-sewed traditional pieces in order to keep their families warm. Today's quilters draw from both sources. They've established a new genre of art.

Betty Busby
Willowmoon | 2008

Twenty years ago, the issue of whether quilting should be considered an art or a craft was a big question. Today, as more and more artists choose the challenges of working with fabric, the issue amuses more than it perplexes. The art quilt movement has changed the way we think about the medium. Art quilts force viewers to move beyond traditional concerns—whether points match, for instance, or stitches are even—and they've introduced a new vocabulary to the quilt world. Words like image, form, line, and composition now claim equal importance with the words color, material, and technique. Avant-garde methods like photo-transfer, raw-edge appliqué, discharging, over-dyeing, faux felting, and stamping are now employed as frequently as more traditional techniques. Without a doubt, the art-quilt movement has fostered artistic innovation and diversity in the quilting world.

Within the realm of art quilts, representational pieces may be accepted more readily by viewers, but it's the abstract creations that force people to look at the medium with fresh eyes. An ancient concept, abstract art that is non-representational and non-figurative draws from both Jewish and Islamic cultures. Many quilt artists also make use of figurative abstractions, eliminating all details and retaining only the essence of a shape or a figure to evoke imagination and emotion. The goal with this type of work is to remove all distractions, so that the energy and spirit of the art can speak clearly to the viewer.

Art quilts frequently convey the essence of non-visual concepts like spirituality, sound, and emotion. Art quilters often show multiple points of view simultaneously, feature the illusion of depth, or make use of negative space in their pieces. Makers of art quilts use the medium to communicate their ideas and beliefs.

Defying modern inclinations, many contemporary art quilters produce representational pieces, and a number of figurative works—quilts depicting animals, flowers, trees, and people—are included here. Some artists are faithful to the size and substance of the subject at hand; others make use of exaggerated colors and scale.

Because of their tactile nature, quilts lend themselves to the depiction of places and scenes. Art quilters are able to capture the qualities of oceans, rivers, lakes, and waves, the topography of land, the architecture of buildings, and the extremes of heat, snow, frost, and ice. Like artists throughout the ages, they deal with the challenge of conveying light—sunlight and moonlight, the glare of summer, and mysterious shadows on snow—in their work.

Art quilts reflect their makers' fascination with fabric—with texture, color, sheen, and weave. Fabric engages the imagination of these artists, and it stirs their curiosity: how can a material be changed to suit a specific purpose? What would the fabric look like rusted? Overdyed or ruched? Layered with transparency? Bleached or painted? Many artists take it a step further: They print and dye their own fabrics, or they incorporate used materials from thrift-shop garments. One quilter I know likes re-using old garments, because the fabrics come with what she calls a "hidden life," a history she knows nothing about.

To me, each of the art quilts in this book comes with a hidden life—a life that is ours to interpret and enjoy. The pieces on these pages are imagination personified. Choosing them was challenging and gratifying, and I am happy to share them with you.

Karey Patterson Bresenhan, *Juror*

Karen Goetzinger
Alpha City 10 | 2008

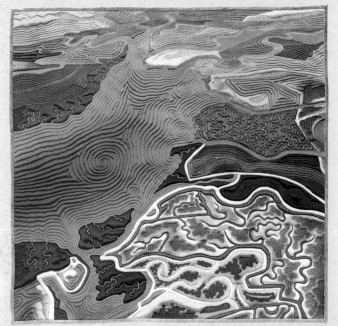

THE QUILTS

Pat Kumicich

The Eyes Have It | 2005

51 X 51 INCHES (129.5 X 129.5 CM)

Cotton, beads, tulle, paint; machine pieced,
hand appliquéd, machine quilted

PHOTO BY ARTIST

Jen Swearington

The Sea Dream | 2008

46 X 44 INCHES (116.8 X 111.8 CM)

Bedsheets, silk, gesso, shellac, ink, charcoal;
machine pieced, machine quilted

PHOTO BY ARTIST

Ann Harwell

Looking for Heaven on Earth | 2006

52 X 37 INCHES (132.1 X 94.0 CM)

Cotton; machine pieced, machine quilted

PHOTOS BY LYNN RUCK

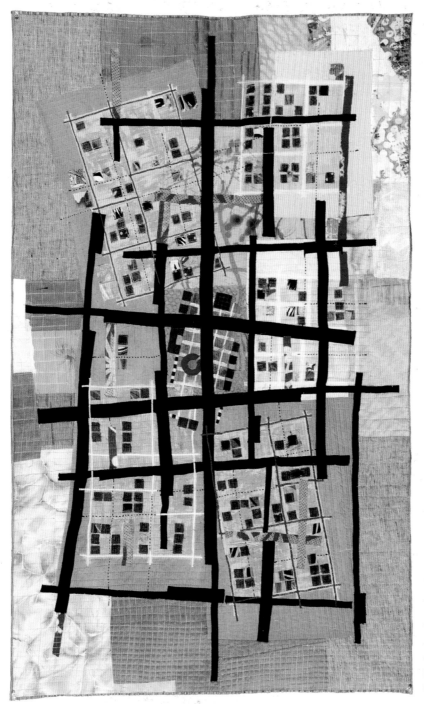

Valerie S. Goodwin
City Grid III | 2007
44 X 32 INCHES (111.8 X 81.3 CM)
Cotton, sheers, paint, thread;
machine quilted, hand stitched
PHOTO BY RICHARD BRUNCK

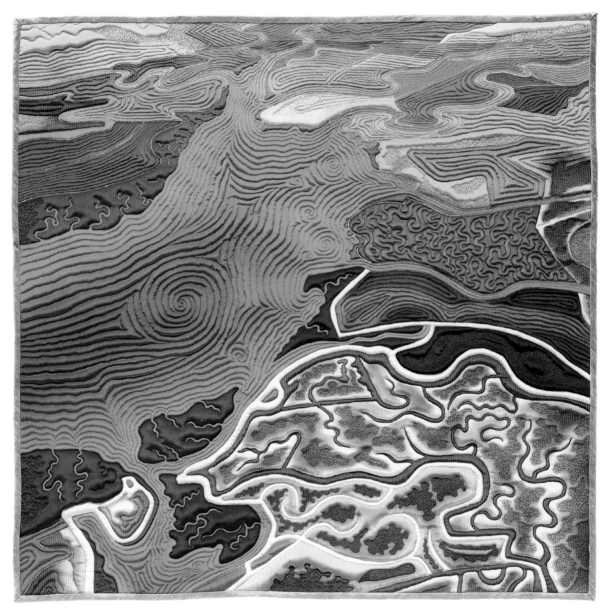

Linda Gass

South Bay | 2006

29 X 29³/₄ INCHES (73.7 X 75.6 CM)

Silk, paint; machine quilted

PHOTOS BY ARTIST

Kathy York

Little Cities | 2006

97 X 96 INCHES (246.4 X 243.8 CM)

Cotton; hand dyed, appliquéd, painted,
machine pieced, machine quilted

PHOTO BY ARTIST

Carol Watkins

Lady of the Wood: Liberation | 2008

34 X 53 INCHES (86.4 X 134.6 CM)

Cotton, synthetics, silk, sequins, beads,
digitally processed photographs; printed, pieced,
appliquéd, free-motion stitched

PHOTOS BY KEN SANVILLE

Judy Coates Perez

Moon Garden | 2008

56 X 69 INCHES (142.2 X 175.3 CM)

Cotton, wool batting, textile paint; machine quilted

PHOTOS BY TOM VAN EYNDE

Reverse Side

Misik Kim

The Wall | 2004

106 X 102 INCHES (269.2 X 259.1 CM)

Fabric; hand dyed, machine pieced, appliquéd, hand quilted

PHOTO BY MANHONG LEE

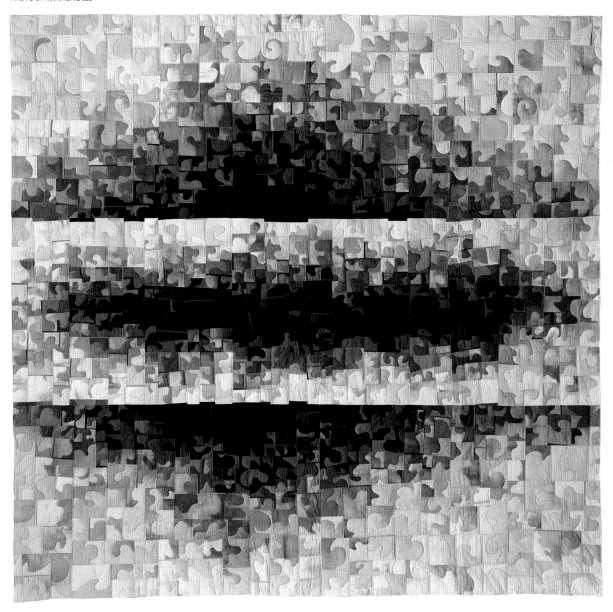

Deborah Sylvester

Evening | 2008

34^1/$_2$ X 34^1/$_2$ INCHES (87.6 X 87.6 CM)

Cotton; machine pieced, appliquéd, machine quilted

PHOTO BY ARTIST

Sherry D. Shine

Friendship | 2007

42 X 42 INCHES (106.7 X 106.7 CM)

Acrylic, cotton; machine quilted

PHOTO BY MARCUS SHINE

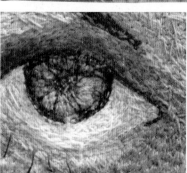

Lora Rocke

Kathryn, Kathy, Katie, Kate | 2007

14 X 16 INCHES (35.6 X 40.6 CM)

Cotton, wool, buttons, glass beads; hand appliquéd, hand stitched, machine quilted

PHOTOS BY ARTIST

Ellen Lindner

Reconciliation | 2006

23 X 22 INCHES (58.4 X 55.9 CM)

Cotton, silk, permanent marker;
raw-edge collaged, machine quilted

PHOTO BY ARTIST

Marilyn H. Wall

A Touch of Red | 2007

41 X 41 INCHES (104.1 X 104.1 CM)

Cotton, silk, beads; fused appliqué,
machine-thread painted, machine quilted

PHOTO BY KERMIT WALL

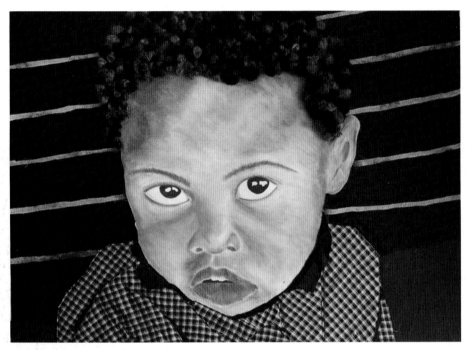

Lynne Morin

Abandoned | 2008

23 X 31 INCHES (58.4 X 78.8 CM)

Cotton, acrylic paint, wire, wool, hair;
machine appliquéd, machine quilted,
hand woven

PHOTO BY ARTIST

Susan V. Polansky

Exuberance | 2006

43 X 88 INCHES (109.2 X 223.5 CM)

Cotton; hand painted, collaged, fused,
machine quilted, hand embroidered

PHOTO BY CLEMENTS/HOWCROFT PHOTOGRAPHY

Lenore Crawford

Pont-en-Royans | 2007

43 X 34 INCHES (109.2 X 86.4 CM)

Fabric, fabric paint; fused, top stitched

PHOTO BY CLINT BURHANS

Terry Waldron

Rain or Shine | 2003

44 X 37 INCHES (111.8 X 94.0 CM)

Cotton, glass beads, thread; hand dyed, hand pieced, hand appliquéd, hand quilted, hand beaded, woven

PHOTOS BY ARTIST

Marcia Stein

'52 Pickup | 2003

42 X 61 INCHES (106.7 X 154.9 CM)

Cotton, lamé, tulle, textile paint; hand dyed,
machine appliquéd, machine pieced, machine quilted

Vita Marie Lovett

Primitive Door Series #32: Hidden Hinge | 2007

18 X 20 INCHES (45.7 X 50.8 CM)

Canvas, acrylic; machine quilted, machine thread painted

PHOTO BY ARTIST

Christine L. Adams

Celebration | 1999

31 X 28 INCHES (78.7 X 71.1 CM)

Silk, cotton, beads, rayon thread, metallic thread;
free-motion quilted, woven

PHOTO BY PAUL-RICARDO S. ELBO

Alessandra Billingslea

Pink Boots | 2008

23 1/2 X 35 INCHES (59.7 X 88.9 CM)

Cotton, yarn; raw-edge appliquéd,
machine quilted

PHOTO BY ARTIST

Liz Alpert Fay

I Spy with My Little Eye, All of Us at Home Inside | 1998

76 X 87 1/2 INCHES (193.0 X 222.3 CM)

Cotton, wool, burlap, gold lamé, cotton batting; reverse appliquéd, painted, beaded, couched, embroidered, hand quilted, hand tied

PHOTOS BY BRAD STANTON

Terry Kramzar

Ravens Return | 2008

60 X 60 INCHES (152.4 X 152.4 CM)

Cotton; hand dyed, machine appliquéd, fused, machine quilted

PHOTO BY ARTIST

Avril Douglas

City Line 2/Colouring Book | 2008

34 X 48 INCHES (86 X 123 CM)

Cotton, embroidery thread; discharged, printed, painted,
reverse appliquéd, hand quilted, embroidered

PHOTOS BY ROGER LEE

Robin Schwalb

Noo Yawk, Noo Yawk | 2006

38 X 36 INCHES (96.5 X 91.4 CM)

Cotton; stenciled, silk-screened, machine pieced,
hand appliquéd, hand quilted

PHOTO BY KAREN BELL

The quilt depicts a postage stamp reading:

SWEAT of the SUN

U.S. 3¢

GOLD CENTENNIAL 1848-1948

TEARS OF THE MOON

SILVER CENTENNIAL 1859-1959

U.S. 4¢

Teresa Barkley

Sweat of the Sun, Tears of the Moon | 1989

64 X 64 INCHES (162.5 X 162.5 CM)

Cotton, polyester, rayon, silk, metallic yarn, braid trim, piping, snaps, acrylic paint; machine pieced, appliquéd, hand quilted

PHOTO BY KAREN BELL

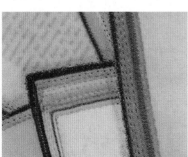

Beatrix von der Heiden

My World in Black and White—Books | 2003

28 X 25 INCHES (71.1 X 63.5 CM)

Cotton, lace; machine pieced, appliquéd, quilted, machine couched

PHOTOS BY ARTIST

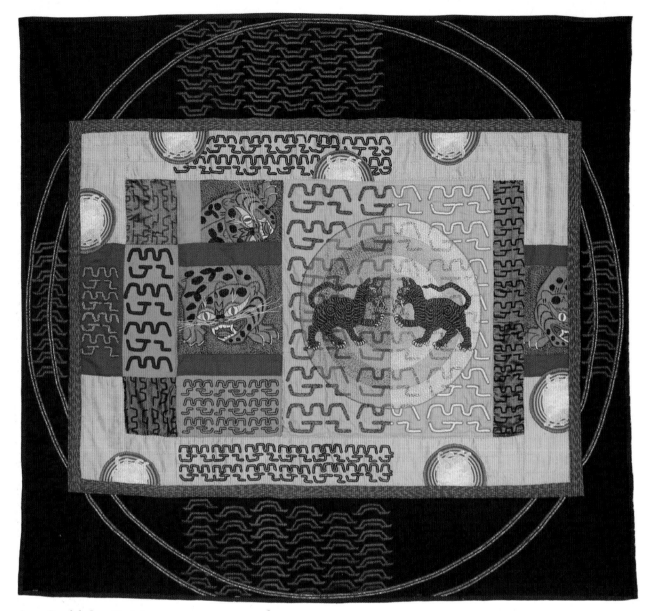

Ann Baddeley Keister

Tooth and Nail | 2008

53 X 58 INCHES (134.6 X 147.3 CM)

Silk, cotton, beads; digital printing, embroidery, machine appliquéd, machine pieced, hand quilted

PHOTO BY ARTIST

Robin Schwalb

Beijing | 2003

77 X 85 INCHES (195.6 X 215.9 CM)

Cotton; stenciled, appliquéd, machine pieced, hand quilted

PHOTO BY KAREN BELL

Ann Kowaleski

Midlife Musings | 1999

44 X 60 INCHES (111.8 X 152.4 CM)

Cotton, silk, vintage fabric, textile paint, buttons, found objects; crocheted, appliquéd, hand quilted, embroidered

PHOTO BY PEGGY BRISBANE

Carol Drummond

Keeping the Faith | 1996

52 X 42 INCHES (132.1 X 106.7 CM)

Cotton, flannel, metallics, silk, found objects; appliquéd, hand quilted

PHOTO BY RICK DRUMMOND

Shawn Quinlan

The Quilt That Won't Comfort | 2002

67 X 18 INCHES (170.2 X 45.7 CM)

Commercial fabric; hand painted, photo transferred

PHOTOS BY ARTIST

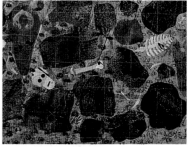

Natasha Kempers-Cullen
Heart of Lightness | 1995
63 X 48 INCHES (160.0 X 121.9 CM)
Fabric, rayon thread, metallic thread, semi-precious stones, glass seed beads, bugle beads, tulle; hand painted, hand printed, collaged, machine stitched, machine quilted, hand beaded

PHOTOS BY DENNIS GRIGGS

Lisa Binkley

Recapitulata (Echo Flower) | 2002

23 X 23¹/₄ INCHES (28.4 X 59.1 CM)

Cotton, beads; machine appliquéd, machine pieced, machine embroidered, hand beaded, hand embroidered, hand quilted

PHOTOS BY EDWARD BINKLEY

Bernie Rowell

Recycled—Future Fossil Four | 2000

52 X 52 INCHES (132.1 X 132.1 CM)

Cotton canvas, metallic fabric, beads, microchips, disk drives, computer boards; hand painted, machine pieced, quilted

PHOTO BY TIM BARNWELL

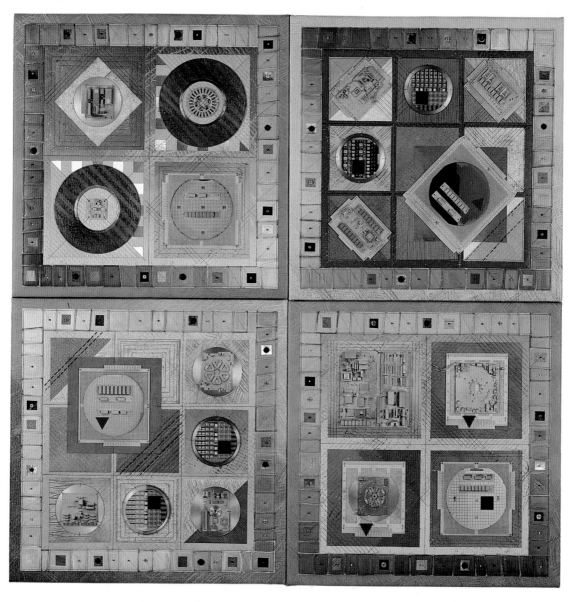

Pamela Thiele

"You decide." "No, you decide." | 2006

58 X 58 INCHES (147.3 X 147.3 CM)

Cotton; machine pieced, machine quilted

PHOTO BY MARCIA WARD

Julie A. Schlueter

Flamenco | 2004

42 X 23 INCHES (106.7 X 58.4 CM)

Cotton, silk, netting, organza, fringe; overdyed, pieced, fused, machine quilted

PHOTOS BY ARTIST

Marianne Burr

Cherry Salsa | 2006

45 X 35 INCHES (114.3 X 88.9 CM)

Silk; hand painted, hand stitched, hand appliquéd

PHOTO BY FRANK ROSS

Sally Dillon

Silk on Silk:
The History of the Silk Industry
in Northampton | 2003

74 X 60 INCHES (188.0 X 152.4 CM)

Silk; hand painted, hand quilted

PHOTO BY STAN SHERER

LM Wood

Fashioned with Patience | 2000

36 X 20 INCHES (91.4 X 50.8 CM)

Cotton, felt, digitally manipulated image;
inkjet printed, pieced, machine quilted

PHOTO BY ARTIST

Shawna Lampi-Legaree

Cause and Effect | 2006

58¹/₂ X 39 INCHES (148.6 X 99.1 CM)

Cotton, silk thread; hand dyed, machine appliquéd, machine quilted, inked

PHOTO BY BOB WILSON

49

Emily Parson
Sunflowers | 2005
83 X 68 INCHES (210.8 X 172.7 CM)
Cotton; hand dyed, fused, machine
appliquéd, machine quilted
PHOTOS BY ARTIST

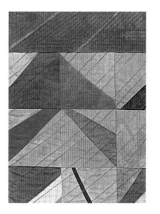

Janet Steadman
Flight Plan | 2006
51 X 48 INCHES (129.5 X 121.9 CM)
Cotton; hand dyed, machine pieced,
machine quilted
PHOTOS BY FRANK ROSS

Desiree Dianne Habicht
Crepe Paper Poppies | 2006
48 X 75 INCHES (121.9 X 190.5 CM)
Fabric, ink, beads, crystals, yarn;
hand painted, thread worked, sewn
PHOTO BY ARTIST

Shirley Jo Rimkus-Falconer

The Milkshakers | 2004

39 1/2 X 52 1/4 INCHES (100.3 X 133.4 CM)

Commercial fabric, cotton batting; machine pieced, appliquéd,
machine embroidered, glued, machine quilted, hand quilted

PHOTOS BY C. DAVID FALCONER

Marguerite J. Lacy
Running Wild—Beautiful World | 2008
41 X 59 INCHES (104.1 X 149.9 CM)
Cotton, crinkle organza, rhinestones; appliquéd,
pieced, machine quilted
PHOTOS BY ARTIST

Mary Arnold
Field of Tulips | 2007
41 X 41 INCHES (104.1 X 104.4 CM)
Cotton sateen, commercial fabric, batiks,
beads; hand dyed, machine appliquéd,
machine quilted
PHOTOS BY MARK FREY

Juanita G. Yeager
Poppies on Purple | 2007
53 X 45 INCHES (134.6 X 114.3 CM)
Cotton, fabric markers, fabric paint; hand dyed, machine pieced, machine appliquéd, thread worked
PHOTO BY ARTIST

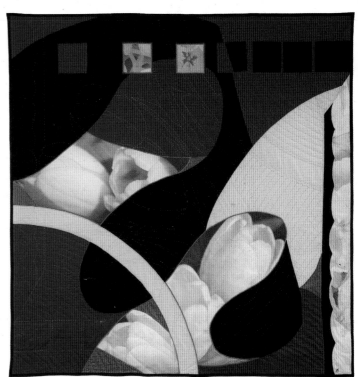

Ann Trusty
Tulips and Matisse | 2008
60 X 60 INCHES (152.4 X 152.4 CM)
Cotton; hand dyed, inkjet printed, machine appliquéd, stitched, hand quilted
PHOTO BY ARTIST

Jan Rickman

The Harvest | 2005

26 X 37³/₄ INCHES (66.0 X 95.9 CM)

Cotton, rayon thread; hand dyed, appliquéd, free-motion machine thread painted, machine quilted

PHOTO BY ARTIST

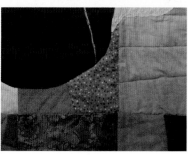

Sharon Breckner

Backyard Ball Game | 2008

43 X 68 INCHES (109.2 X 172.7 CM)

Cotton; pieced, appliquéd, machine quilted

PHOTOS BY BOB BRECKNER

Mary Jo Bowers

An Abandoned Barn | 2008

18¹/₂ X 20 INCHES (47.0 X 52.1 CM)

Cotton; hand dyed,
raw-edge machine appliquéd,
machine quilted

PHOTO BY PETER JONES

David Taylor

I Ain't No Spring Chicken! | 2007

39 X 57 INCHES (99.1 X 144.8 CM)

Commercial prints, fabric; hand dyed, machine pieced,
machine appliquéd, machine quilted

PHOTOS BY ARTIST

Holly Knott

Buttercup | 2005

45 X 20 INCHES (114.3 X 50.8 CM)

Cotton, textile paint, tulle;
machine appliquéd, machine quilted

PHOTO BY ARTIST

Philippa Naylor
Star Sign | 2007

89 X 89 INCHES (226.1 X 226.1 CM)

Cotton; hand dyed, pieced, trapunto,
free-motion quilted

PHOTOS BY LINDA TEUFEL

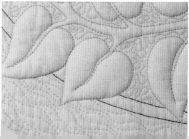

Yvonne Porcella

Dick and Jane | 2007

53 X 68 INCHES (134.6 X 172.7 CM)

Cotton, silk; fused, machine stitched

PHOTO BY DAVID LUTZ

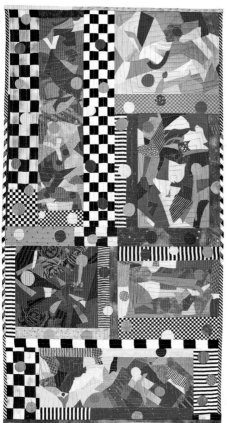

Cynthia Lockhart
Dance of Hope | 2006
70 X 60 INCHES (177.8 X 152.4 CM)

Mixed textiles, leather, suede, braid trim,
stones, brass hardware; hand quilted,
machine quilted French-bias edged,
draped, appliquéd

PHOTO BY JAY YOCIS

Cynthia H. Catlin

Dancing Through the Storm | 2005

32 X 24 INCHES (81.3 X 61.0 CM)

Cotton, silk, beads, crystals;
machine appliquéd, machine quilted

PHOTO BY ROBERT CATLIN

Carol Ann Waugh
Ladies Who Lunch | 2007
59 X 49 INCHES (149.8 X 124.5 CM)
Cotton, beads, ribbon, metal, flowers, screen, roving, doll's hair, feathers; machine stitched

PHOTO BY KEN SANVILLE

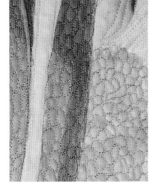

Carol Morrissey

Lily | 2008

36 X 48 INCHES (91.4 X 121.9 CM)

Cotton, textile ink, paint; machine
appliquéd, machine quilted

PHOTOS BY ARTIST

Susan K. Willen

*Fitting It All In
(An Homage to Betty Friedan
and Wendy Wasserstein)* | 2006

36 X 60 INCHES (91.4 X 152.4 CM)

Cotton; hand dyed, machine pieced,
machine quilted

PHOTO BY ARTIST

Andrea M. Brokenshire

Dahlia Delight | 2008

34 X 33¹/₂ INCHES (86.4 X 85.1 CM)

Cotton, silk, rayon/polyester thread, fusible web; raw-edge
machine appliquéd, machine quilted, thread painted

PHOTO BY ROY PEÑA

Marilyn Belford

My Parents | 2000

21 X 27 INCHES (53.3 X 68.6 CM)

Cotton; machine appliquéd, machine quilted

PHOTO BY STEPHEN APPEL

Deborah Sylvester
A Moment in the Shadows | 2005
32 X 56 INCHES (81.3 X 142.2 CM)
Cotton; appliquéd, machine pieced,
machine quilted
PHOTO BY ARTIST

Marilyn Henrion
Disturbances 7 | 2005
66 X 65 INCHES (167.6 X 165.1 CM)
Silk; hand pieced, hand quilted
PHOTO BY KAREN BELL

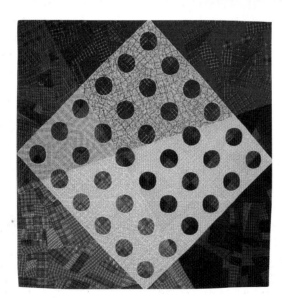

Ruby Horansky
Overtones | 2008
45³/₄ X 45³/₄ INCHES (116.2 X 116.2 CM)
Cotton, cotton blends; machine pieced,
machine quilted, bobbin embroidered
PHOTO BY ARTIST

Jane Sassaman

Minor Miracle | 1999

48 X 30 INCHES (121.9 X 76.2 CM)

Cotton; machine appliquéd, machine quilted

PHOTOS BY GREGORY GAUTNER

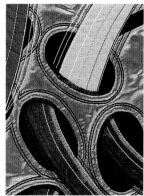

Anne Lullie

Fiesta Floribunda II | 2004

49 X 50 INCHES (124.5 X 127.0 CM)

Cotton, fusible appliqué; hand dyed,
hand embroidered, machine quilted

PHOTOS BY ARTIST

Shelly Pagliai

Purr-sian Delight: Miss Kitty's Garden | 2007

28 X 39 INCHES (71.1 X 99.1 CM)

Cotton; hand dyed, hand appliquéd, hand quilted

PHOTO BY ARTIST

Shirley H. MacGregor

Fish II | 2004

30 X 31½ INCHES (76.2 X 80.0 CM)

Cotton, synthetic fabric, sheer polyester fabric;
appliquéd, machine quilted, free floated

PHOTO BY DON FERGUSON

Scott A. Murkin

Strata XVII: Water Garden | 2006

58 X 38 INCHES (147.3 X 96.5 CM)

Cotton, rayon, polyester, beads;
machine pieced, machine quilted,
hand beaded

PHOTO BY ARTIST

Sally Dillon

Seadragons | 2006

72 X 60 INCHES (182.9 X 152.4 CM)

Silk; hand painted, hand quilted

PHOTOS BY JOHN POLAK

Sarah Ann Smith

Koi | 2007

57 X 41 INCHES (144.8 X 104.1 CM)

Cotton, batik, fusible web, paint, beads, thread,
synthetic sheer fabric; hand dyed, hand appliquéd,
machine appliquéd, trapunto, beaded

PHOTO BY ARTIST

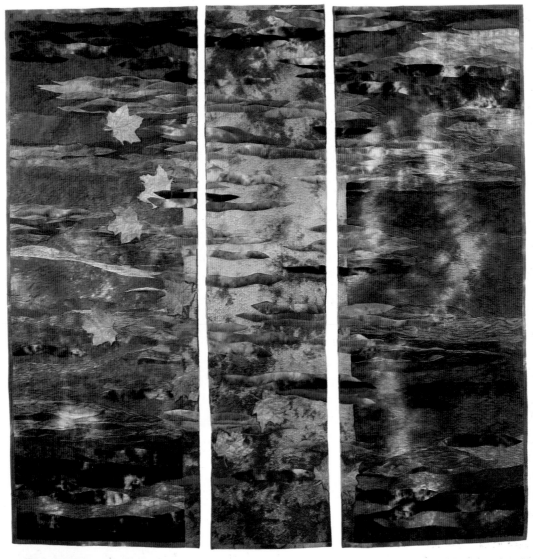

Shelley Brucar

Floating Leaves Revisited | 2007

62 X 60 INCHES (157.5 X 152.4 CM)

Cotton, silk, velvet; hand dyed, raw-edge appliquéd, machine quilted

PHOTOS BY ARTIST

Jen Swearington
Off Nantucket | 2008
29 X 27 INCHÈS (73.7 X 68.6 CM)
Vintage domestic textiles, silk, gesso, shellac, ink, charcoal,
thread; machine pieced, machine quilted, hand embroidered
PHOTO BY ARTIST

Ginny Eckley
City Birds | 2007
50 X 43 INCHES (127.0 X 109.2 CM)
Silk, fabric; silk-screened, dyed,
painted, printed
PHOTO BY RICK WELLS

Teresa Shippy

Women of Substance | 2007

19 X 22¹/₂ INCHES (48.3 X 57.2 CM)

Cotton, acrylic paint, varnish, embroidery thread;
machine quilted, hand painted, stenciled

PHOTO BY ARTIST

Marilyn Belford

Rundy | 2005

51 X 41 INCHES (129.5 X 104.1 CM)

Cotton; machine appliquéd, machine quilted

PHOTOS BY STEPHEN APPEL

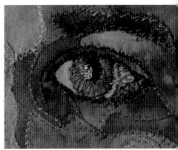

Patricia Gould

Four Strong Winds | 2008

48 X 60 INCHES (121.9 X 152.4 CM)

Cotton, silk binding; hand painted, photo printed,
free-motion machine quilted

PHOTO BY ARTIST

Barbara Barrick McKie

One Good Tern Deserves Another | 2008

18 X 45½ INCHES (45.7 X 115.6 CM)

Cotton, wool batting, polyester crepe; disperse dyed,
hand dyed, trapunto, machine appliquéd, machine quilted

PHOTO BY ARTIST

Kathy Angel Lee

Marsh River | 2007

10 X 25 INCHES (25.4 X 63.5 CM)

Cotton, silk ribbon, rayon thread; machine appliquéd,
machine quilted, thread painted

PHOTOS BY ARTIST

Dottie Moore

Invisible Forces | 2008

39 X 66 INCHES (99.1 X 167.6 CM)

Cotton; hand painted, machine
appliquéd, machine quilted,
hand embroidered

PHOTO BY MICHAEL HARRISON

Marjan Kluepfel

Monterey Cypress | 2008

37 X 29 INCHES (94.0 X 73.7 CM)

Cotton, thread; hand dyed, machine quilted

PHOTO BY ARTIST

Carol Ann Waugh

Please Save the Earth | 2008

52 X 49 INCHES (132.1 X 124.5 CM)

Fabric; inkjet printed, hand painted, fused, machine stitched

PHOTO BY KEN SANVILLE

Mary Ruth Smith
Off the Rack | 2008
17 X 18 INCHES (43.2 X 45.7 CM)
Cotton; pieced, hand stitched
PHOTO BY ARTIST

Charlotte Ziebarth

Reflection/Ripples View #1 | 2008

49 X 43 INCHES (124.5 X 109.2 CM)

Silk, pigment inks, digitally manipulated photographs; appliquéd; free-motion machine quilted

PHOTOS BY ARTIST

Gwyned Trefethen

Botswana Bounty | 2008

30 X 30 INCHES (76.2 X 76.2 CM)

Cotton; machine pieced, machine appliquéd, machine quilted

PHOTO BY JOE OFRIA

Deborah Fell

Serendipity Duet 3 | 2008

34 X 58 INCHES (86.4 X 147.3 CM)

Fiber-reactive dye, cotton, textile paint, foil, canvas;
screen-printed, immersion dyed, raw-edge appliquéd,
fused, pieced, machine quilted

PHOTO BY ARTIST

Rhoda E. Taylor

Pretzels and Champagne | 2008

46 X 40 INCHES (116.8 X 101.6 CM)

Cotton, commercial fabrics; discharged, arashi shibori,
scrunched, machine pieced, machine quilted

PHOTO BY ARTIST

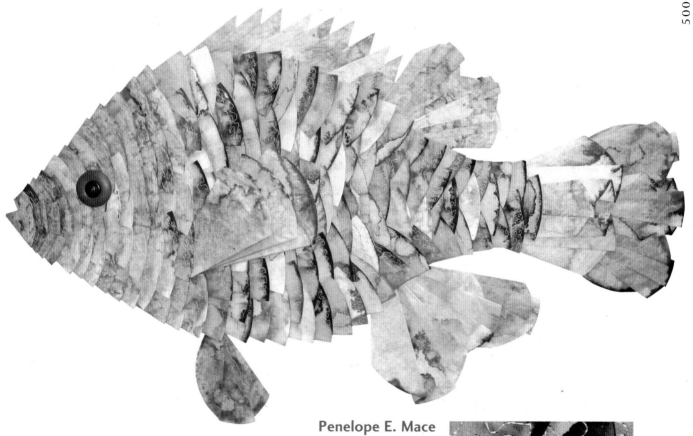

Penelope E. Mace

Hooked on Caffeine | 2008

33¹/₂ X 50¹/₂ INCHES (85.1 X 128.3 CM)

Coffee filters, cotton, metallic thread, cotton
thread, buttons; machine quilted, hand quilted,
hand appliquéd

PHOTOS BY WILLIAM F. GOSSMAN

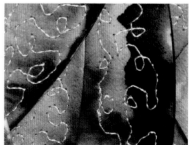

Rosalie Baker

You Are My Sunshine | 2006

61 X 51 INCHES (154.9 X 129.5 CM)

Cotton; machine pieced, appliquéd, hand painted, machine quilted

PHOTOS BY ARTIST

Kathy McNeil

Gone Fishin' | 2007

72 X 64¹/₂ INCHES (182.9 X 163.8 CM)

Recycled denim shirt, cotton; hand appliquéd, machine appliquéd, hand dyed, machine quilted

PHOTOS BY BRUCE MCNEIL

Brenda H. Smith
Wildfire! | 2005
54 X 41 INCHES (137.2 X 104.1 CM)
Cotton; hand dyed, thermo-screened,
digitally printed, machine pieced,
machine quilted
PHOTOS BY ARTIST

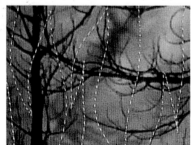

Phyllis Cullen

Sunset Tree | 2006

36 X 44 INCHES (91.4 X 111.8 CM)

Cotton, organza, wool, acrylic, metallic novelty yarn, cord; machine appliquéd, couched, embroidered, quilted, hand dyed

PHOTOS BY ARTIST

Denise Oyama Miller

Roadside Poppies | 2008

26 X 35 INCHES (66.0 X 88.9 CM)

Cotton, fusible web; painted, inked,
fused, machine quilted

PHOTO BY ARTIST

Ellen Lindner

Ti Plants A-Glow-Glow | 2008

24¹/₂ X 36 INCHES (62.2 X 91.4 CM)

Cotton; raw-edge collaged,
machine quilted

PHOTO BY ARTIST

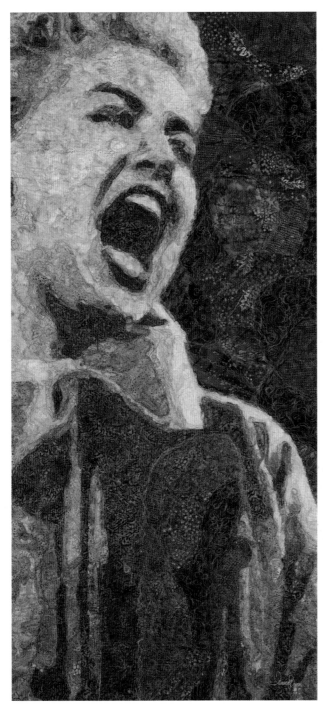

Tammie Bowser

Song | 2005

58 X 27 INCHES (147.3 X 68.6 CM)

Cotton; machine quilted

PHOTOS BY ARTIST

Gloria Hansen

Blushing Triangles 4 | 2008

41¹⁄₂ X 40¹⁄₂ INCHES (105.4 X 102.9 CM)

Silk, cotton, pigment ink, fabric paint, fabric pastels;
machine pieced, machine quilted

PHOTO BY ARTIST

MaryLou Pepe

Careers Abound I—The Investment | 2005

72 X 132 INCHES (182.9 X 335.3 CM)

Cotton sateen, novelty cotton fabrics, polyester batting;
hand painted, hand silk-screened, hand stenciled,
hand block printed, machine embroidered, machine appliquéd,
machine quilted, machine pieced

PHOTO BY ARTIST

Jeannette DeNicolis Meyer

Full Circle | 2003

32 X 44¹/₂ INCHES (81.2 X 113 CM)

Cotton; hand dyed, discharged, machine pieced,
machine quilted, hand embroidered

PHOTO BY BILL BACHHUBER

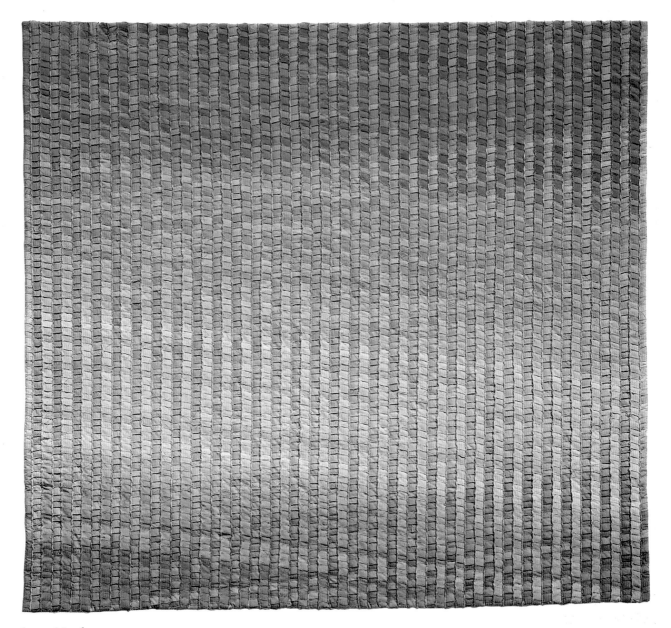

Inge Hueber

High Tide/Low Tide—Broadstairs, Kent | 2007

64 X 70 INCHES (162.6 X 177.8 CM)

Cotton; hand dyed, machine pieced, machine quilted

PHOTO BY ROLAND HUEBER

Dominie Nash

Stills from a Life | 2006

82 X 82 INCHES (208 X 208 CM)

Cotton, silk organza; machine appliquéd, quilted

PHOTO BY MARK GULEZIAN

Robin Schwalb

Chinese Characters | 2006

67 X 93 INCHES (170.2 X 236.2 CM)

Cotton; stenciled, silk-screened, appliquéd, machine pieced, hand quilted

PHOTOS BY KAREN BELL

Meri Henriques Vahl

Las Mujeres Azules de Guatemala (The Blue Ladies of Guatemala) | 2007

44 X 60 INCHES (111.8 X 152.4 CM)

Guatemalan cotton, cotton batiks, muslin;
hand appliquéd, machine quilted

PHOTOS BY ARTIST

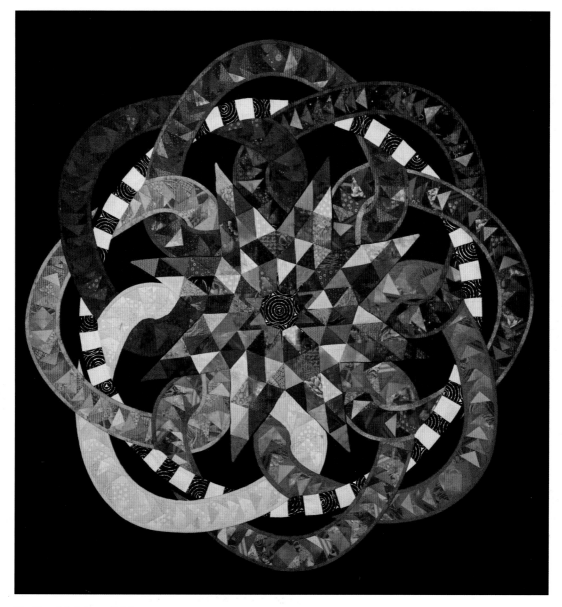

Kathy Lichtendahl

One Single Color (Does Not a Rainbow Make) | 2004

36 X 36 INCHES (91.4 X 91.4 CM)

Cotton; hand dyed, machine pieced, machine quilted

PHOTO BY ARTIST

Denise Tallon Havlan

Unbridled Passion | 2006

51 X 49 INCHES (129.5 X 124.5 CM)

Cotton, crystals, oil sticks, colored pencil, textile paint;
machine appliquéd, hand appliquéd, machine quilted

PHOTO BY ARTIST

Linda Barlow

The Road to . . . Happiness? | 2007

71 X 45 INCHES (180.3 X 114.3 CM)

Cotton; dyed, painted, printed, pieced, appliquéd, hand quilted, machine quilted

PHOTOS BY ARTIST

Deborah K. Snider

Ancestories: Welsh Memories | 2007

40 X 40 INCHES (101.6 X 101.6 CM)

Cotton; raw-edge appliquéd, free-motion machine quilted

PHOTO BY FRANK NORED

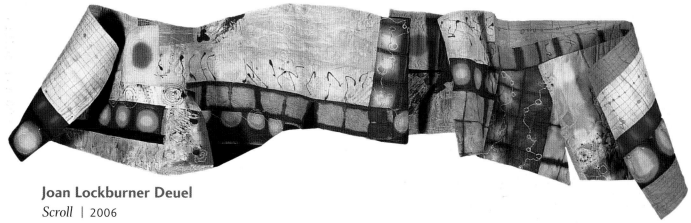

Joan Lockburner Deuel
Scroll | 2006
16 X 59 INCHES (40.6 X 149.9 CM)
Cotton; dyed, painted, machine quilted
PHOTO BY ANDREW GILLIS

Eileen Klee Sweeney
Dancing with the Moons | 2005
13 X 27 INCHES (33.0 X 68.6 CM)
Cotton, cotton floss; hand dyed, fused,
embroidered
PHOTOS BY ARTIST

Mary Ellen Heus

Great Balls of Fire | 2004

57 1/2 X 35 1/2 INCHES (146.1 X 90.2 CM)

Cotton, pearl cotton, paint, foil,
cotton/polyester batting; dyed,
painted, couched, machine pieced,
appliquéd, quilted

PHOTO BY ANTHONY HEUS

Barbara Olson
Prismatic Flowers | 2004
71 X 71 INCHES (180.3 X 180.3 CM)
Commercial fabric; hand dyed, machine
appliquéd, machine quilted
PHOTO BY PHOTOGRAPHIC SOLUTIONS

Deborah Fisher

Fantastic Voyage | 2008

86 X 64 INCHES (218.4 X 162.6 CM)

Cotton; machine pieced, machine quilted, hand appliquéd, hand embroidered

PHOTO BY ARTIST

Ruth A. White

A Nebulous Affair | 2004

38¹/₂ X 38¹/₂ INCHES (97.8 X 97.8 CM)

Cotton velveteen, silk organza, silk, rayon thread, Swarovski crystals; hand dyed, machine quilted

PHOTOS BY ANDREW GILLIS OF CASCADILLA PHOTOGRAPHY

Barbara Shapel
Moonlight Sonata | 2007
63 X 39 INCHES (160.0 X 99.1 CM)
Cotton, silk; machine appliquéd,
machine quilted
PHOTO BY MARK FREY

Kathy McNeil
Spring Rituals | 2007
42 X 66 INCHES (106.7 X 167.6 CM)
Thai silk, silk organza; hand appliquéd,
machine sashiko
PHOTO BY BRUCE MCNEIL

Marilyn Farquhar
Having a Sip | 2007
48 X 59 INCHES (121.9 X 149.9 CM)
Cotton; hand appliquéd,
machine quilted
PHOTO BY ARTIST

Chiaki Dosho

Sumie—Cherry Blossom Wind | 2008

57 X 78 INCHES (144.8 X 198.1 CM)

Silk, Chinese ink; machine appliquéd,
hand embroidered, painted

PHOTOS BY TOSHIHIRO KOBE

Wendy Butler Berns

Reflections of God's Skin | 2004

73 X 44 INCHES (185.4 X 111.8 CM)

Cotton, rayon thread, collage elements;
machine embellished, machine quilted

PHOTO BY ARTIST

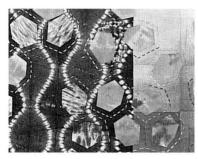

Harumi Iida

Puzzled Bees | 2007

52¹/₂ X 73 INCHES (133.3 X 185.4 CM)

Cotton, indigo, chemicals; hand dyed, machine pieced,
hand appliquéd, hand quilted

PHOTOS BY FUMIO TAKAHASHI

Casey Puetz

Serenity | 2008

19¹/₂ X 14¹/₈ INCHES (49.5 X 35.9 CM)

Cotton, polyester, Timtex,
silk cocoons, glass beads; raw-edge
appliquéd, machine quilted

PHOTO BY WILLIAM LEMKE

Mark Sherman

Wisteria | 2008

84 X 59 INCHES (213.4 X 149.9 CM)

Cotton; hand dyed, turned-edge machine appliquéd, machine quilted

PHOTOS BY MARK WOODBURY, WOODBURY & ASSOCIATES PHOTOGRAPHY

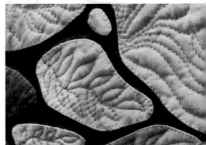

Bonnie J. Smith
View From Above | 2008
43 X 41 INCHES (109.2 X 104.1 CM)
Cotton, silk fabric; machine appliquéd,
machine quilted
PHOTO BY GREGORY CASE

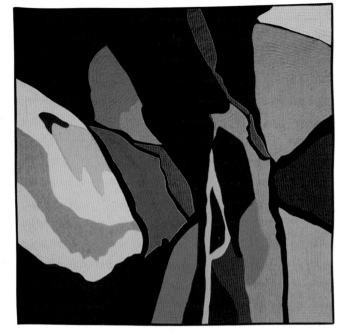

Diana Bracy
"The Duke"—Duke Ellington | 2008
15 X 22 INCHES (38.1 X 55.9 CM)
Cotton, fusible tricot; hand fused
PHOTO BY ARTIST

Sylvia Weir
Man at Ease | 2007
20 X 18 INCHES (50.8 X 45.7 CM)
Cotton, silk; screen-printed, machine appliquéd,
thread sketched
PHOTO BY ARTIST

Margot Lovinger

Afternoon | 2007

30 X 50 INCHES (76.2 X 152.4 CM)

Cotton, tulle, beads; hand sewn, hand embroidered,
hand beaded

PHOTO BY ARTIST

Heidi Field-Alvarez

Young Catherine | 2008

16 X 12 INCHES (40.6 X 30.5 CM)

Canvas, cotton, cotton
embroidery floss, silver floss;
digitally transferred, hand
painted, hand appliquéd,
trapunto, hand embroidered

PHOTO BY ARTIST

123

Sandra Hoefner

The Day Before Pearl Harbor I | 2004

61 X 38 INCHES (154.9 X 96.5 CM)

Cotton, piping, buttons;
hand appliquéd, quilted

PHOTOS BY VICTOR C. HOEFNER III

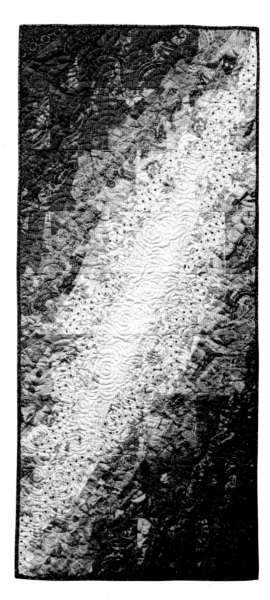

Libby Mijanovich
Jim Mijanovich
Autumn Path I & II | 200
33¹/₂ X 32 INCHES (85.1 X 81.3 CM)
Vintage cotton clothing, metallic thread;
hand-guided machine quilted
PHOTO BY ARTISTS

Lori Lupe Pelish

Curtain Call for Aphrodite | 2005

47 X 40 INCHES (119.4 X 101.6 CM)

Cotton; machine appliquéd, machine quilted,
machine embroidered, knotted

PHOTO BY DAVID PELISH

Mary Diamond

Quartet, Four Pieces | 2007

EACH PIECE 37 X 24 INCHES (94.0 X 61.0 CM)

Cotton, silk, synthetics, beads, fiber; hand dyed, hand appliquéd, raw-edge machine appliquéd, machine quilted, hand embellished

PHOTO BY AVEC LANGRIDGE, CAYUGA COLOR LAB

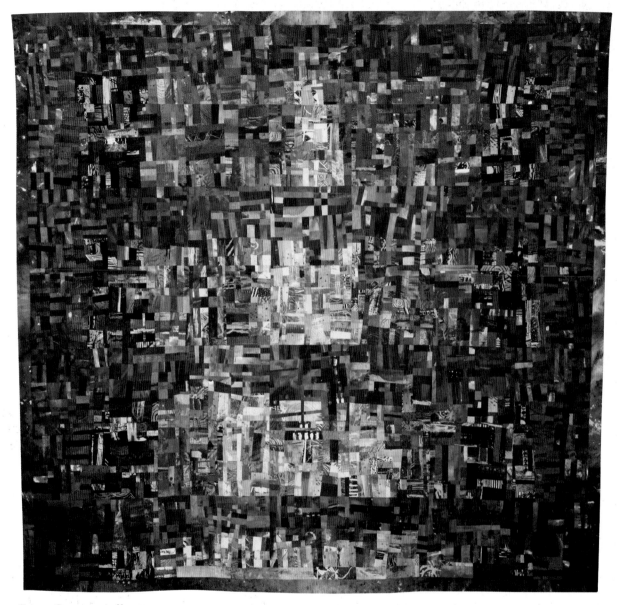

Fran Cowen Adler

Both Ends Burning | 2008

64 X 67 INCHES (162.6 X 170.2 CM)

Cotton; hand dyed, hand painted, machine quilted, hand embroidered

PHOTO BY AMIRE GAMZU

Melinda Bula
Social Climber Roses | 2005
34 X 48 INCHES (86.4 X 121.9 CM)
Cotton, rayon thread, fusible
appliqué; machine quilted
PHOTOS BY ARTIST

Ann Miller Maley

Garden Trellis | 2007

104 X 96 INCHES (264.2 X 243.8 CM)

Cotton; machine appliquéd, machine pieced, machine quilted

PHOTO BY ROBERT SCHELLHAMMER

Leela Cherian

Two Pots | 2005

FRAMED, 57¹/₂ X 36¹/₂ INCHES (146.1 X 92.7 CM)

Cotton, silk, lace, beads; hand dyed, appliquéd,
free-machine quilted, sculpted

PHOTO BY TORSTEN BORCHERS

Melinda Bula

A Garden's Delight | 2005

57 X 44 INCHES (144.8 X 111.8 CM)

Cotton, rayon thread, fusible appliqué;
machine quilted

PHOTO BY ARTIST

131

Marjan Kluepfel

Ménage à Trois | 2008

46 X 51 INCHES (116.8 X 129.5 CM)

Cotton; hand dyed, fused, machine quilted

PHOTO BY ARTIST

Karen Goetzinger

Building Over the Past | 2008

48 X 60 INCHES (121.9 X 152.4 CM)

Cotton, silk, gold foil, glass beads, resistors, acrylic paint; machine pieced, raw-edge appliquéd, machine quilted, hand embroidered

PHOTOS BY ARTIST

Sherry D. Shine
Waiting on Momma | 2006
24 X 24 INCHES (61.0 X 61.0 CM)
Acrylic, cotton; machine quilted
PHOTO BY MARCUS SHINE

Suzanne Mouton Riggio
Stormy Weather | 2004
58 X 37 INCHES (147.3 X 94.0 CM)
Cotton, polyester, synthetic suede, paint;
machine appliquéd, machine quilted, fused,
painted, computer printed
PHOTO BY ARTIST

Ellie Kreneck
Deanna | 2007
53 X 36 INCHES (134.6 X 91.4 CM)
Cotton, dye; painted,
machine pieced, hand appliquéd,
hand quilted
PHOTOS BY ARTIST

Barbara Otto
River Valley #1 | 1995
53 X 37 INCHES (134.6 X 94.0 CM)
Cotton, whole cloth;
dye painted, machine quilted
PHOTO BY ARTIST

Barbara Lange

Astronomical Clock of Lyon | 2007

63 X 49 INCHES (160.0 X 124.5 CM)

Cotton, velvet, beads; machine pieced, machine quilted, machine embroidered

PHOTO BY ARTIST

Carol Taylor
Revolutions | 2002
55 X 47 1/2 INCHES (139.7 X 120.7 CM)
Cotton sateen; hand dyed, pieced, machine quilted
PHOTOS BY ARTIST

Karen Goetzinger

Alpha City 10 | 2008

48 X 24 INCHES (121.9 X 61.0 CM)

Cotton, silk, copper tape, resistors, metal, acrylic paint; raw-edge appliquéd, machine quilted, free-motion stitched

PHOTOS BY ARTIST

Karen Colbourne Martin

Three Sheets to the Wind | 2005

18 X 26 INCHES (45.7 X 66 CM)

Cotton, synthetics; hand appliquéd, machine construction

PHOTO BY ARTIST

Jane Dunnewold

Guide 1 | 2007

54 X 60 INCHES (137.2 X 152.4 CM)

Silk broadcloth; resisted, dyed, screen-printed, pieced, needle felted

PHOTO BY PATRICIA ESPINOSA

Charlotte Bird

Labyrinth 3: A Lifetime of Imagination | 2006

56 X 56 INCHES (142.2 X 142.2 CM)

Cotton, nylon organza, monofilament, polyester thread,
polyester batting, wood, electric rice lights, plastic grid, wire,
table, hook-and-loop tape; hand dyed, hand printed,
hand cut, die cut, appliquéd, machine quilted

PHOTO BY JACK YONN

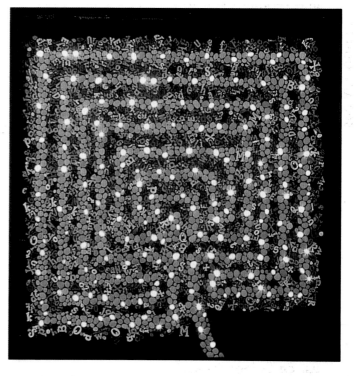

Marcia Stein

Window Shopping | 2007

51 X 34 INCHES (129.5 X 86.4 CM)

Cotton; hand dyed, machine appliquéd,
machine pieced, machine quilted

PHOTO BY ARTIST

Darlene Garstecki

The Lotus | 2007

48 X 83 INCHES (121.9 X 210.8 CM)

Cotton, silk, beads; hand painted, free-motion embroidered, machine pieced, machine quilted

PHOTOS BY ARTIST

Marilyn Fromherz
Koi Pond at Sunset | 2008
34 X 24 INCHES (86.4 X 61.0 CM)
Cotton; machine appliquéd,
machine quilted, beaded
PHOTOS BY ARTIST

143

Donna Cherry
Moonlight Goddess | 2006
47 X 28 INCHES (119.4 X 71.1 CM)
Cotton, organza, rayon floss, beads, tulle, metallic
thread; hand appliquéd, machine pieced, trapunto,
hand embroidered, free-motion machine quilted

PHOTOS BY ARTIST

Kathleen W. Connor

Peak-A-Boo Parrotfish | 2008

9 X 12 INCHES (22.9 X 30.5 CM)

Cotton, felt, luminescent fiber, rhinestone, earring, tulle, merino wool, soy silk, wool batting, cotton backing, binding; ironed, glued, hand dyed, hand painted, machine appliquéd, machine felted, embellished, cut, free-motion machine quilted

PHOTOS BY ARTIST

Desiree Dianne Habicht

Transformations | 2006

38$^1/_2$ X 53 INCHES (97.7 X 134.6 CM)

Fabric, fabric markers, ink; hand painted, hand dyed, appliquéd, quilted

PHOTOS BY ARTIST

Alice Fuchs Garrard

As Spring Unfolds | 2001

65 X 65 INCHES (165.1 X 165.1 CM)

Cotton; machine pieced, quilted

PHOTO BY ARTIST

Leigh Elking

Water's Edge | 2006

24 X 23 INCHES (61.0 X 58.4 CM)

Cotton, organza, paint, ink, polyester, metallic thread, beads, cord;
printed, appliquéd, hand knitted, beaded, machine quilted

PHOTO BY ARTIST

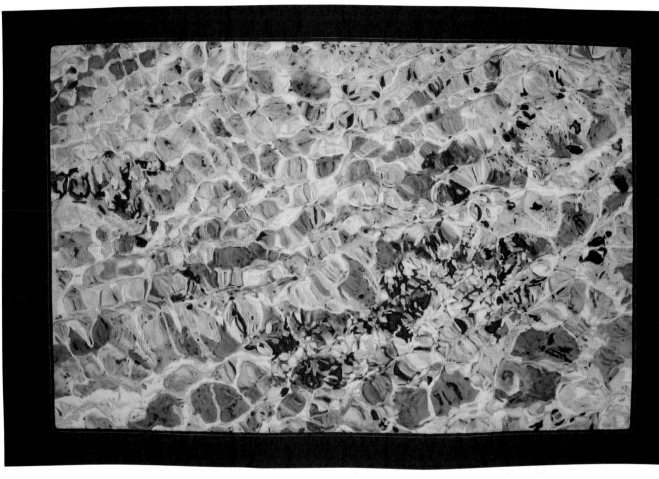

Melissa K. Frankel
Water on Cement with Pebbles:
Detail of the Los Angeles River | 2006
29 X 45 INCHES (73.7 X 114.3 CM)
Silk, cotton batting, watercolor pencil, pastels; machine appliquéd, quilted
PHOTO BY ARTIST

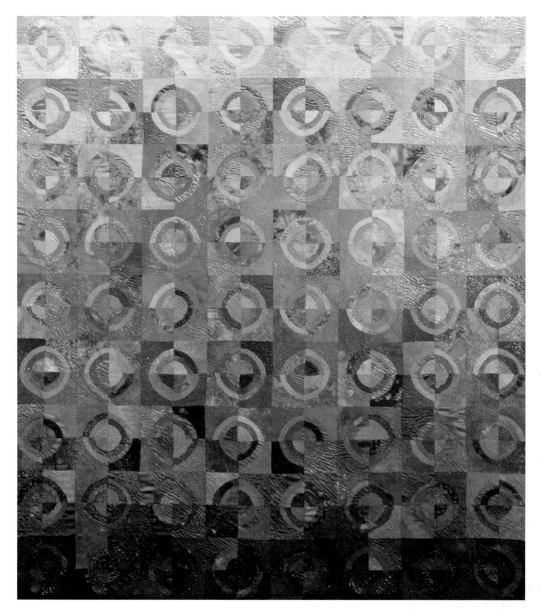

Susan Leslie Lumsden

Seeking Clarity | 2006

63 X 56 INCHES (160.0 X 142.2 CM)

Cotton, silk, foil, metallic thread, textile pigments;
hand dyed, machine appliquéd, machine pieced

PHOTO BY ARTIST

Nelda Warkentin

Palmaceae | 2004

40 X 60 INCHES (101.6 X 152.4 CM)

Silk, cotton, canvas; painted

PHOTO BY JOHN TUCKEY

Brenda Gael Smith

Grass | 2007

38 X 59 INCHES (96.5 X 149.9 CM)

Cotton; hand dyed, machine
pieced, machine quilted

PHOTO BY ARTIST

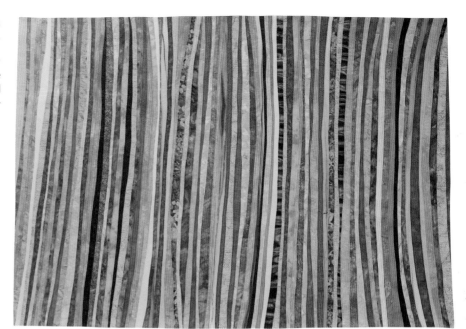

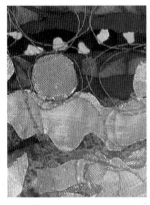

Alison Muir

The Four-Year Term | 2005

51 X 142 INCHES (129.5 X 360.7 CM)

Silk, metal, polyester, fusible appliqué; hand dyed, machine quilted

PHOTOS BY ANDREW PAYNE

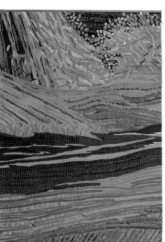

151

Margit Kagerer

Shapes over Blue and Purple | 2008

29 X 25 INCHES (73.7 X 63.5 CM)

Cotton, acetate, polyester; machine stitched, cut

PHOTO BY HEINZ KAGERER

Margarete Steinhauer

Tsunami | 2005

43 X 41 INCHES (109.2 X 104.1 CM)

Cotton, beads; machine pieced, hand appliquéd, machine quilted, hand beaded

PHOTO BY JOE OFRIA

Barbara J. Schneider

Reflections, Brushy Creek, Kansas City, MO, Var. 7 | 2004

46¹/₂ X 35 INCHES (115.6 X 88.9 CM)

Cotton; hand dyed, fused, machine stitched

PHOTO BY ARTIST

Alison Muir

Hidden Depths | 2004

43 X 42 INCHES (109.2 X 106.7 CM)

Commercial silk, fusible appliqué, digital collage;
machine quilted

PHOTO BY ANDREW PAYNE

Elizabeth Barton
Shadow with Five Diamonds | 2007
46 X 26 INCHES (116.8 X 66 CM)
Cotton; hand dyed, machine pieced
PHOTO BY ARTIST

Diane W. Smith

Indian River Sunset | 2003

42 X 53 INCHES (106.7 X 134.6 CM)

Cotton, images; hand dyed, fused, machine quilted

PHOTO BY ARTIST

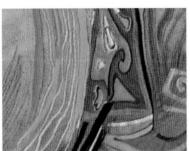

Valentyna Roenko Simpson

The New Beginning of an Ancient World | 2004

42 X 66 INCHES (106.7 X 167.6 CM)

Silk, velvet; hand painted, appliquéd, machine quilted

PHOTOS BY ARTIST

Mary Jo Bowers

It Is 5 O'Clock Somewhere | 2008

45 X 41 INCHES (114.3 X 104.1 CM)

Cotton, silk, synthetic fabric; hand dyed,
raw-edge appliquéd, machine embroidered

PHOTO BY ARTIST

MaryLou Pepe

Careers Abound II—The Return | 2007

72 X 132 INCHES (182.9 X 335.3 CM)

Cotton sateen, novelty cotton fabrics, polyester batting; hand painted, hand silk-screened, hand stenciled, hand block printed, machine embroidered, machine appliquéd, machine quilted, machine pieced

PHOTOS BY ARTIST

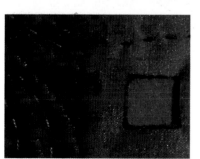

Jamie Fingal

Living Out Loud | 2008

26¹/₂ X 37¹/₂ INCHES (67.3 X 95.3 CM)

Wool felt, zippers, silk, velvet, beads, grommets, snaps, ring trim, washers, safety pins; block printed, machine quilted, embroidered

PHOTOS BY ARTIST

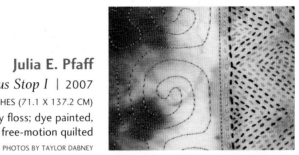

Julia E. Pfaff

My Year at the Bus Stop I | 2007

28 X 54 INCHES (71.1 X 137.2 CM)

Cotton, cotton embroidery floss; dye painted,
hand embroidered, machine pieced, free-motion quilted

PHOTOS BY TAYLOR DABNEY

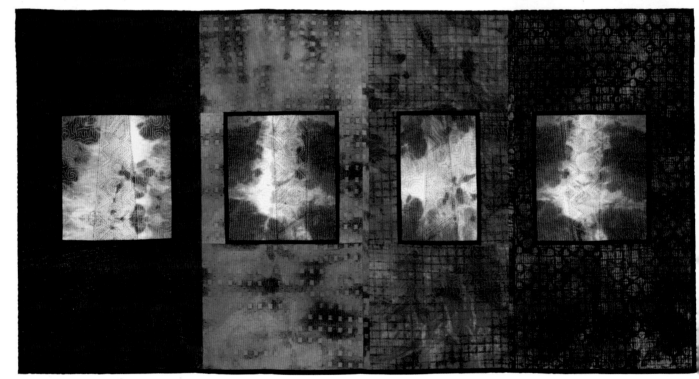

Helen Remick

Spinning Out Spinning In 1 | 2006

58 X 71 INCHES (147.3 X 180.3 CM)

Cotton, cotton/polyester batting, paper; machine pieced,
hand appliquéd, hand couched, machine quilted

PHOTO BY MARK FREY

Gabrielle Paquin
Scarlet Ibis | 2006
65 X 47 INCHES (165.1 X 119.4 CM)
Cotton, linen; machine appliquéd,
machine quilted
PHOTO BY DENIS TRIMOREAU

Wendy F. Strumwasser

Crazy for Me! | 2003

43 X 44 INCHES (109.2 X 111.8 CM)

Cotton, seed beads; hand embellished, machine quilted

PHOTO BY LARRY H. STRUMWASSER

Leslie Rego
Summer Hues | 2005
28 X 21 INCHES (71.1 X 53.3 CM)
Cotton, metallic silk; hand
dyed, machine embroidered,
machine quilted
PHOTO BY F. ALFREDO REGO

Constance Norton

Dawn's Early Light | 2005

58 X 43 INCHES (147.3 X 109.2 CM)

Cotton; machine pieced,
machine quilted

PHOTO BY CHICO

Donna Cherry

Grand Canyon Monarch | 2007

63 X 42 INCHES (160.0 X 106.7 CM)

Cotton, tulle, organza, yarn, paint sticks, puff paint, textile ink; hand dyed, machine pieced, hand appliquéd, bobbin stitched, trapunto, machine embroidered, hand embroidered, free-motion machine quilted

PHOTOS BY ARTIST

Margaret A. Phillips

Uncle Mike | 2008

12 X 12 INCHES (30.5 X 30.5 CM)

Cotton; hand dyed, appliquéd, machine quilted

PHOTO BY ARTIST

Clara Lawrence

Beaming with Pride | 2008

26 X 28 1/2 INCHES (66.0 X 71.1 CM)

Cotton, dye; hand painted, machine quilted

PHOTOS BY ARTIST

Renée M. Allen

Hallelujah | 2005

48 X 50 INCHES (121.9 X 127.0 CM)

Cotton, beads, paint, ribbon; hand appliquéd,
hand embroidered, hand quilted

PHOTO BY ARTIST

Lenore Crawford

Bronwyn's Garden | 2006

42 X 28 INCHES (106.7 X 71.1 CM)

Fabric, fabric dye; painted, appliquéd, top stitched

PHOTO BY CLINT BURHANS

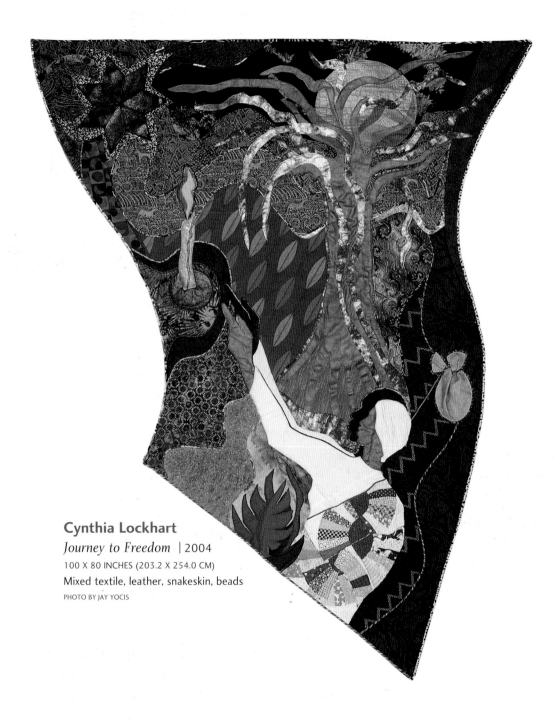

Cynthia Lockhart
Journey to Freedom | 2004
100 X 80 INCHES (203.2 X 254.0 CM)
Mixed textile, leather, snakeskin, beads
PHOTO BY JAY YOCIS

Mary Ev Wyatt

The Potato Series: Remembering 1847 | 2008

38 X 33 INCHES (96.5 X 83.8 CM)

Fabric, image transfers; printed, discharged,
hand quilted, machine quilted

PHOTO BY G.R. WYATT

Janet Kurjan
Underwater Reflection | 2004
80 X 40 INCHES (203.2 X 101.6 CM)
Cotton; machine quilted
PHOTO BY MARK FREY

Judith Content
Acqua Chiara | 2008
63 X 50 INCHES (160.0 X 127.0 CM)
Thai silk; shibori, discharged, pieced,
quilted, appliquéd
PHOTO BY JAMES DEWRANCE

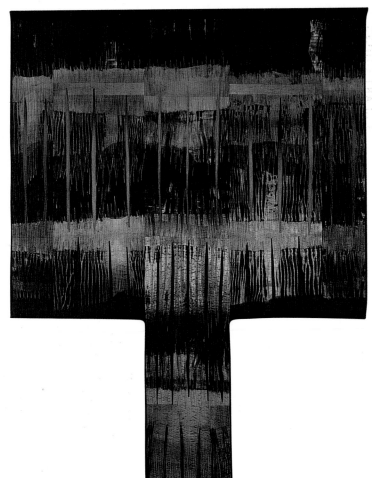

Anne Lullie
Colorplay V | 2006
43 X 25 INCHES (109.2 X 63.5 CM)
Cotton, fusible appliqué; hand dyed,
machine quilted
PHOTO BY ARTIST

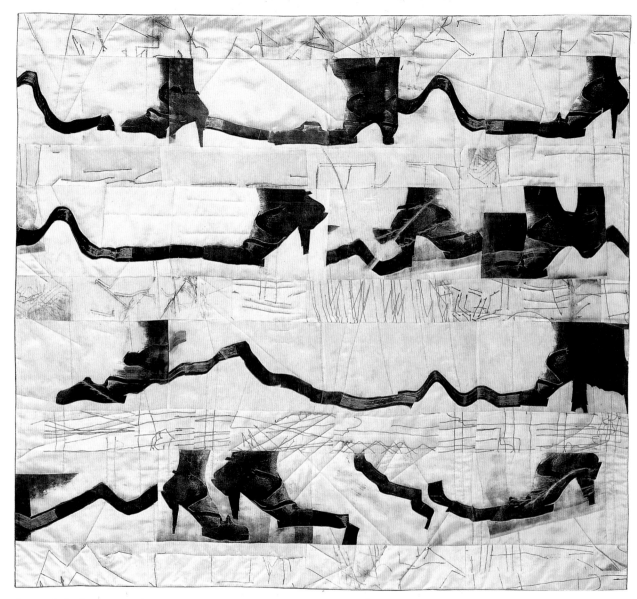

Joan Schulze

Tango | 2008

46¼ X 57½ INCHES (117.5 X 146.1 CM)

Silk; photocopied, direct printed, pieced, machine quilted

PHOTO BY SHARON RISEDORPH

Janet Cooper

Wedding Dress Quilt | 2008

41 X 29 INCHES (104.1 X 73.7 CM)

Vintage fabric, lace, porcelain dolls, vintage paper, hot glue; hand stitched

PHOTO BY LISA VOLLMER

David Taylor
Sally at the Window | 2006
51 X 40 INCHES (129.5 X 101.6 CM)
Commercial prints, fabric;
hand dyed, machine pieced,
machine appliquéd,
machine quilted
PHOTO BY ARTIST

Lonni Rossi

Moon Goddess | 2006

50¹/₄ X 50 INCHES (127.6 X 127.0 CM)

Cotton, luminescent fiber; hand painted, machine appliquéd, machine quilted, machine embroidered

PHOTO BY LIVIJA MCCLAIN

Deborah K. Gregory

Choices and Pathways VIII | 2008

51 X 16 INCHES (129.5 X 40.6 CM)

Cotton; discharged, dyed, painted, machine quilted, hand quilted

PHOTOS BY KEN WAGNER

Alice Leck Gant

The Secret Life of Mother Goose | 2006

72 X 60 INCHES (182.9 X 152.4 CM)

Acrylic, muslin, drapery fabric; painted, machine stitched, neo-reverse appliquéd

PHOTOS BY SHERYL SINKOW

Grace J. Errea

Jessie | 2005

36 X 33 INCHES (91.4 X 83.8 CM)

Cotton; machine appliquéd, machine quilted

PHOTOS BY ARTIST

Laura Fogg
Say It with Flowers | 2007
41 X 49 INCHES (104.1 X 124.5 CM)
Cotton, upholstery fabric, satin, tulle, chenille yarn, digital prints;
machine appliquéd, machine quilted
PHOTO BY ARTIST

Colleen Ansbaugh
Portrait: Warrior | 2008
41¹/₂ X 32 INCHES (105.4 X 81.3 CM)
Cotton; hand dyed, fabric dyed,
overdyed, discharged, machine
appliquéd, machine quilted

PHOTO BY ARTIST

Jo-Ann Golenia

Lucy | 2007

25 X 25 INCHES (63.5 X 63.5 CM)

Cotton, polyester trilobal thread,
fusible appliqué; machine quilted

PHOTOS BY ARTIST

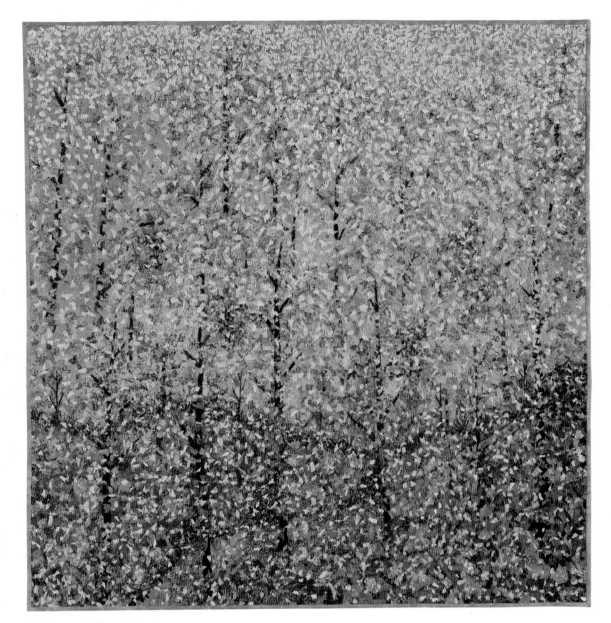

Barbara Oliver Hartman

Falling Leaves | 2008

41 X 40¹/₂ INCHES (104.1 X 102.9 CM)

Cotton; machine appliquéd, machine quilted

Lois Puckett Wilson

Leaves on the Pond | 2002

30 X 44 INCHES (76.2 X 111.8 CM)

Cotton; machine pieced, hand appliquéd, hand quilted, stitched

PHOTO BY LARRY GAWEL

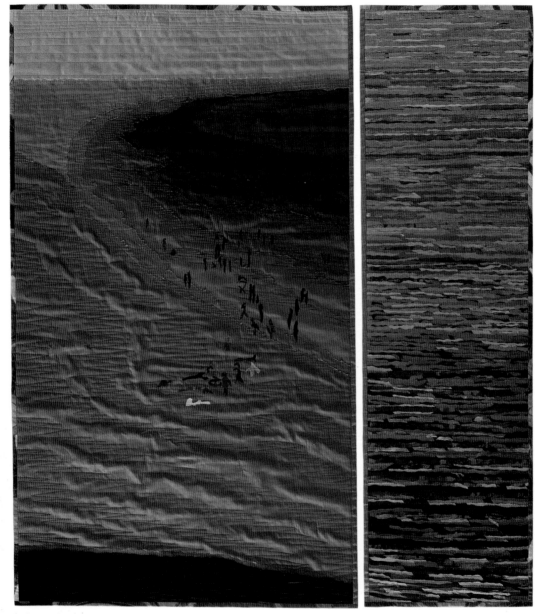

Alison Muir

Summers Passed | 2004

54 X 48 INCHES (137.2 X 121.9 CM)

Commercial silk, paper, fusible appliqué, digital collage; machine quilted

PHOTO BY ANDREW PAYNE

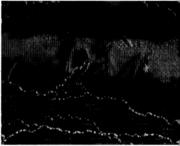

Sue Wademan

Last Light | 2005

18 X 14 INCHES (45.7 X 35.6 CM)

Cotton, silk, synthetic fabric, rayon thread; collaged, layered, free-motion machine stitched

PHOTOS BY HOLLY WALLACE

Joan Sowada

Illumination | 2007

32 X 48 INCHES (81.3 X 121.9 CM)

Cotton, colored pencil, oil pastel sticks; fused,
machine appliquéd, machine quilted

PHOTOS BY DAVID NICHOLAS

Lenore Crawford

A City Walk in Spring | 2008

38¹⁄₂ X 25¹⁄₄ INCHES (97.8 X 64.1 CM)

Fabric, fabric paint; fused,
top stitched

PHOTOS BY CLINT BURHANS

Linda Levin
City with Footnotes VII | 2008
54 X 51 INCHES (137.2 X 129.5 CM)
Cotton, textile paint; machine stitched
PHOTO BY JOE OFRIA

Elizabeth Barton

Gathering Storm | 2006

27 X 44 INCHES (68.6 X 111.8 CM)

Cotton, silk; machine pieced, machine appliquéd, hand stitched, machine stitched, hand dyed, screen-printed

PHOTOS BY ARTIST

Karen Colbourne Martin

As Seen with the Listening Heart | 2003

21¹/₂ X 32¹/₂ INCHES (54.6 X 82.6 CM)

Cotton, synthetics, wool; hand appliquéd,
machine constructed

PHOTOS BY ARTIST

Barbara J. West

Friends in High Places | 2006

54¹/₂ X 36¹/₂ INCHES (138.4 X 92.7 CM)

Silk, cotton, polyester, burlap, wool, beads, acrylic, fabric paint; pieced, appliquéd, embroidered, quilted

PHOTO BY JOSEPH POTTS

Annette M. Hendricks

MoonDance | 2006

47¼ X 51¼ INCHES (120.0 X 130.2 CM)

Cotton; hand dyed, dye painted, appli-pieced,
machine appliquéd, machine quilted, relief quilted

PHOTO BY ARTIST

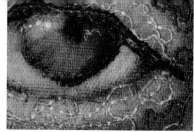

Denise Tallon Havlan

Piegan | 2007

19 X 18 INCHES (48.3 X 45.7 CM)

Cotton, ribbon embellishment, textile paint; machine embroidered, hand appliquéd, machine appliquéd, machine quilted

PHOTOS BY ARTIST

Yesterday I was a dog. Today I am a dog. Tomorrow I'll probably still be a dog. Sigh. There's so little hope for advancement.

Pauline Salzman

Inside There's a Person | 2007

41 X 41 INCHES (104.1 X 104.1 CM)

Cotton, tulle, paint; machine appliquéd, machine quilted

PHOTOS BY ARTIST

Jane Burch Cochran

Legacy | 2007

64 X 77 INCHES (162.6 X 195.6 CM)

Fabric, beads, buttons, pot holders, gloves, bottle caps; crocheted, hand appliquéd, hand quilted, embellished

PHOTOS BY PAM BRAUN

Sarah Ann Smith

A Sense of Place: The Wall | 2007

27 X 29 1/2 INCHES (68.6 X 74.9 CM)

Cotton, fusible web, yarn, thread, fusible collage, fusible appliqué;
hand dyed, free-motion machine quilted, couched

PHOTO BY ARTIST

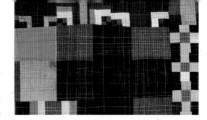

Eleanor A. McCain
9 Patch Color Study 4 | 2007
104 X 91 INCHES (264.2 X 231.1 CM)
Cotton; hand dyed, cut, machine pieced, machine quilted
PHOTOS BY LUKE JORDAN

Jane Burch Cochran

Shroud for a Colorful Soul | 2005

44 X 66 INCHES (111.8 X 167.6 CM)

Fabric, buttons, beads, sequins, paint, found items, gloves; crocheted, hand appliquéd, quilted, embellished, machine patchworked, hand tied

Marion Coleman

Keepers at the Village Gate | 2007

42 X 53 INCHES (106.7 X 134.6 CM)

Mud cloth, African prints, cotton, yarn; fused, machine pieced, machine quilted

PHOTO BY NYLS JONGEWAARD

Sally A. Sellers

HomeBody | 1992

56 X 59 INCHES (142.2 X 149.9 CM)

Cottons, synthetics, velvet, canvas; machine appliquéd

PHOTO BY BILL BACHHUBER

Mary Ruth Smith
All in the Family #1 | 2006
21 X 21 INCHES (53.3 X 53.3 CM)
Cotton; appliquéd, stitched
PHOTO BY ARTIST

Diane Savona
Fossil Strata #2 | 2008
23.5 X 23¹/₂ INCHES (59.7 X 59.7 CM)
Vintage damask napkin, snaps, scissors, wool
batting, fabric; screen-resist printed, batiked,
dyed, hand sewn, discharged
PHOTOS BY ARTIST

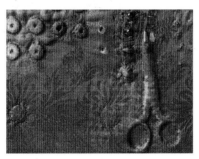

Sylvia H. Einstein

Minstrel | 2004

38 X 37 INCHES (96.5 X 94.0 CM)

Cotton; machine pieced, machine quilted

PHOTO BY DAVID CARAS

Ann Harwell

Colliding Spiral Galaxies | 2007

36 X 65 INCHES (91.4 X 165.1 CM)

Cotton; machine pieced, machine quilted

PHOTOS BY LYNN RUCK

Violet O. Cavazos
Gold Break | 2006
45 X 34 INCHES (114.3 X 86.4 CM)
Cotton; machine pieced,
machine quilted
PHOTO BY CHICO

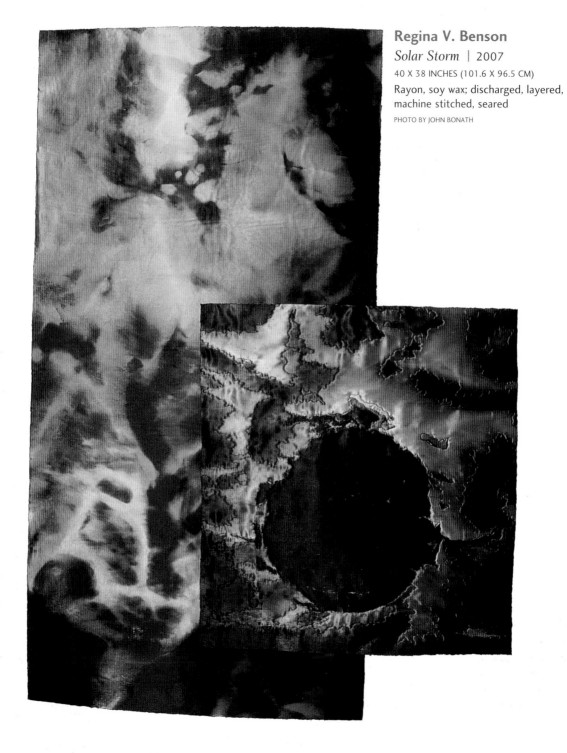

Regina V. Benson
Solar Storm | 2007
40 X 38 INCHES (101.6 X 96.5 CM)
Rayon, soy wax; discharged, layered,
machine stitched, seared
PHOTO BY JOHN BONATH

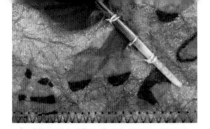

Jessica Elizabeth Jones
Sound | 2006
44 X 27 INCHES (111.8 X 68.6 CM)
Cotton, silk organza, beads; digitally
printed, machine embroidered
PHOTO BY ARTIST

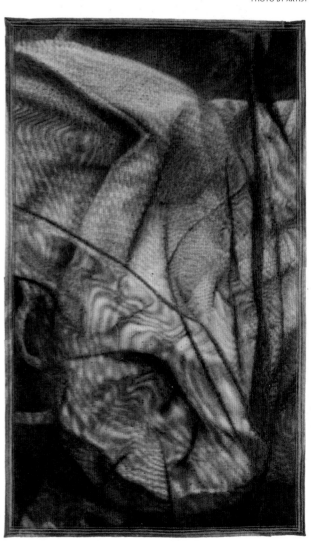

Pat Dolan
Woodland Walk | 2007
25 1/2 X 28 INCHES (64.8 X 71.1 CM)
Fabric, paper, metal mesh, buttons, feathers,
colored pencil; rusted, marbled, stamped,
painted, machine pieced, machine quilted
PHOTOS BY ARTIST

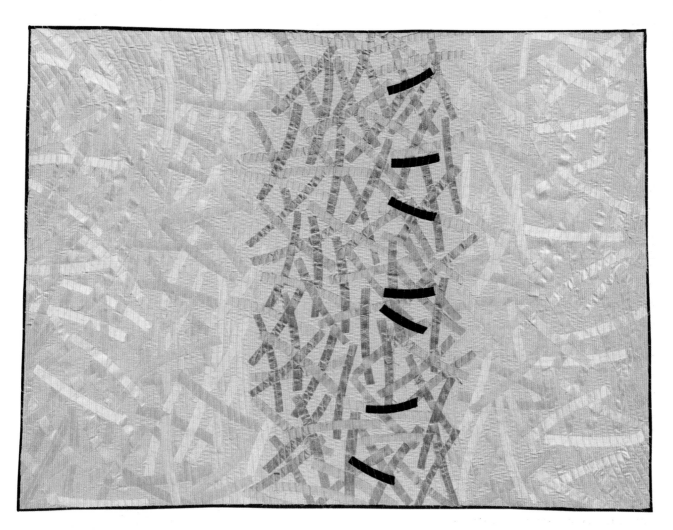

Carmella Karijo Rother

No. 7 | 2007

30 X 40 INCHES (76.2 X 101.6 CM)

Dupioni silk, cotton, mixed fiber, thread, interfacing; machine quilted

PHOTO BY ARTIST

Kent Williams
Around the Bend | 2008
72 X 60 INCHES (182.9 X 152.4 CM)
Cotton; machine pieced,
machine quilted
PHOTOS BY ERIC TADSEN

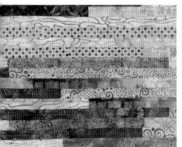

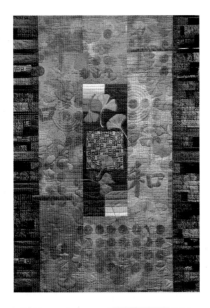

Lonni Rossi

Harmony | 2003

43¼ X 30 INCHES (103.5 X 76.2 CM)

Fabric; hand painted, laser printed, silk-screened, machine appliquéd, machine quilted, machine embroidered

PHOTO BY JUDY SMITH-KRESSLY

Lucinda Carlstrom

Sunshine Crazy Quilts | 2007

EACH 24 X 72½ INCHES (61.0 X 181.6 CM)

Silk, Japanese paper, paste paper, bronze leaf; sewn, machine pieced, hand tied

PHOTO BY ARTIST

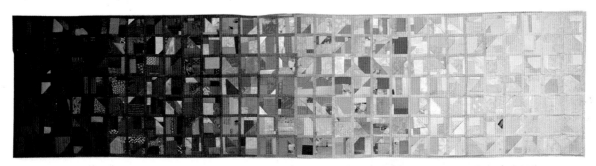

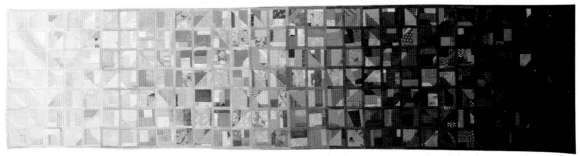

Aryana B. Londir
Desert Heat | 2008
39 X 25 INCHES (99.1 X 63.5 CM)
Cotton; discharged, screen-printed,
machine quilted
PHOTO BY ARTIST

Sue Kongs

Lava Fountains | 2008

59 X 33 INCHES (149.9 X 83.8 CM)

Cotton; fuse appliquéd, machine quilted

PHOTOS BY TOM KONGS

Jean Neblett

Reflections 16: El Rio Grande | 2003

54 X 54 INCHES (137.2 X 137.2 CM)

Cotton, rayon thread; hand dyed, machine appliquéd, machine quilted

PHOTO BY SIBILA SAVAGE

Diane W. Smith
Fire | 2003
45 X 38 INCHES (114.3 X 96.5 CM)
Fabric; hand dyed, woven,
machine quilted
PHOTO BY ARTIST

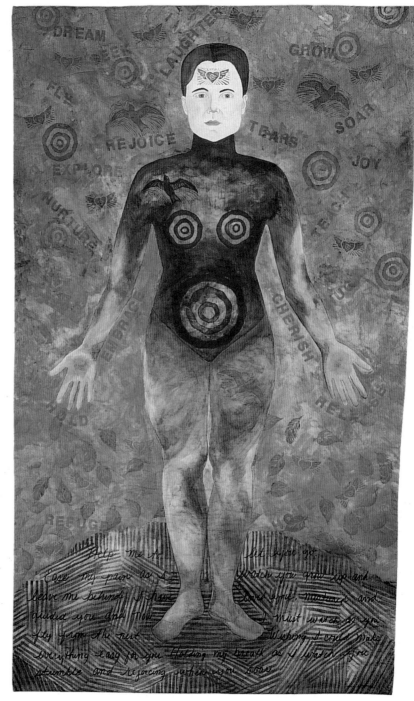

Jill Jensen
Woman I: Letting Go | 2003
71 X 41¹⁄₄ INCHES (180.3 X 104.8 CM)
Cotton, paint; relief printed,
hand quilted
PHOTOS BY ARTIST

Kathy Nida

Lost | 2005

51 X 51 INCHES (129.5 X 129.5 CM)

Cotton; appliquéd, hand dyed, machine stitched, machine quilted

PHOTO BY ARTIST

LM Wood

A Summer's Morning | 2004

40 X 33 INCHES (101.6 X 83.8 CM)

Fabric, cotton sheeting, cotton batting, wool felt, digitally manipulated image; inkjet printed, machine quilted

PHOTO BY ARTIST

Rosalie Baker

Fisherman Jim | 2003

68 X 50 INCHES (172.7 X 127 CM)

Cotton, computer-generated image, paper foundation; machine pieced, hand appliquéd, hand painted, hand quilted, machine quilted

PHOTO BY ARTIST

Susan R. Sorrell

Louie's Dog-Jazz | 2003

12¼ X 13¾ INCHES (31.1 X 34.9 CM)

Cotton, fabric paint, beads,
embroidery floss; hand embroidered,
hand quilted, beaded

PHOTOS BY RODNEY SORRELL

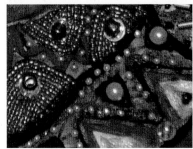

Gay E. Lasher

Cow Pie | 2007

24 X 36 INCHES (61.0 X 91.4 CM)

Commercial fabric, acrylic ink, archival printing inks, digitally printed images; painted, machine quilted, appliquéd

PHOTOS BY JOHN BONATH

Maya Schonenberger

Hindsight | 2008

20 X 20 INCHES (50.8 X 50.8 CM)

Cotton, acrylic paint, paper, printed material;
painted, machine stitched, glued

PHOTO BY WERNER BOEGLIN

Ann Fahl

On the Nile | 2008

45$\frac{1}{2}$ X 62$\frac{1}{2}$ INCHES (115.6 X 158.8 CM)

Cotton; machine pieced, fused,
machine embroidered, appliquéd, quilted

PHOTO BY ARTIST

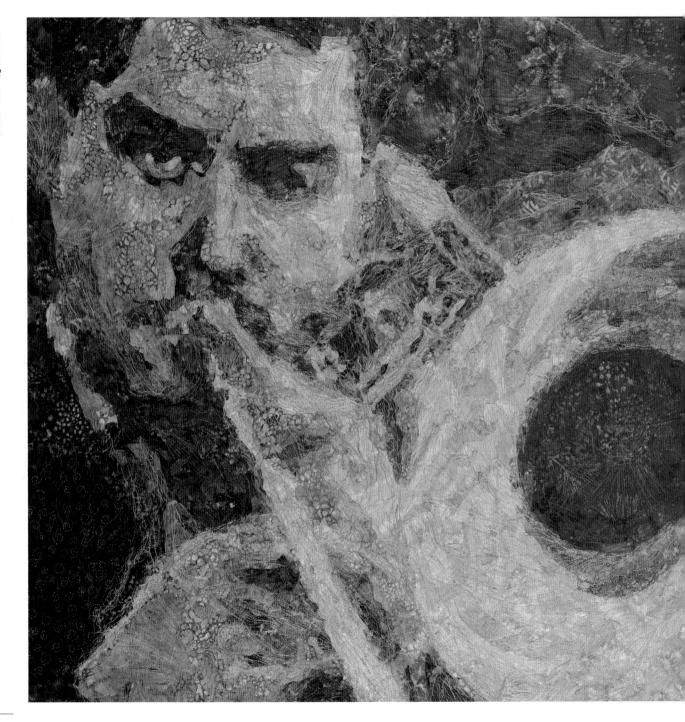

Tammie Bowser
Trombone | 2005
35 X 47 INCHES (88.9 X 119.4 CM)
Cotton; machine quilted
PHOTOS BY ARTIST

Tamar Drucker
The Musicians | 2006
54 X 54 INCHES (137.2 X 137.2 CM)
Cotton, silk; appliquéd, thread painted, machine quilted
PHOTO BY ARTIST

225

Ann E. Ruthsdottir

The Retrospective Theater | 2008

64³/₄ X 41 INCHES (164.5 X 104.1 CM)

Cotton, velveteen, gold lamé, gold paint, permanent markers; pieced, computer printed, raw-edge fused, machine quilted

PHOTO BY ARTIST

Barbara Williamson

Moonlit Garden | 2008

DIAMETER, 31 INCHES (78.7 CM)

Glass, fusible web, fabric, beads, nylon yarn, plastic
canvas yarn, organza, fabric paint; hand dyed,
appliquéd, free-motion stitched, fused, beaded

PHOTO BY ARTIST

Juanita Lanaux

Lady Day | 2003

44½ X 43¾ INCHES (113.0 X 111.1 CM)

Cotton, suede; hand appliquéd, hand quilted

PHOTO BY ARTIST

227

Luella Morgenthaler
Fall Swirl | 2008
39 X 34 INCHES (99.1 X 86.4 CM)
Cotton; painted, fused,
machine quilted
PHOTO BY KEN SANVILLE

Melissa K. Frankel

Magnolia | 2005

30 X 48 INCHES (76.2 X 121.9 CM)

Wool, silk, cotton; hand dyed, machine appliquéd, painted, embroidered

PHOTO BY ARTIST

Barbara Olson

Red Lion Flower | 2006

24 X 29 INCHES (61.0 X 73.7 CM)

Commercial fabric, crystals; hand dyed,
machine appliquéd, machine quilted

PHOTO BY PHOTOGRAPHIC SOLUTIONS

Diane J. Evans

Dizzy | 2006

35 X 35 INCHES (88.9 X 88.9 CM)

Cotton; machine pieced, machine
appliquéd, machine quilted

PHOTO BY ARTIST

Ruth Powers

Watermelon Wine | 2006

69¼ X 55 INCHES (175.9 X 139.7 CM)

Cotton; machine pieced,
machine quilted

PHOTO BY ARTIST

Jenny Hearn
On Thin Ice | 2008
72 X 56 INCHES (182.9 X 142.2 CM)
Cotton, silk, embroidery thread, tapestry wool;
machine pieced, machine appliquéd, machine
quilted, hand embroidered
PHOTOS BY ARTIST

Judith Shevell
Tahiti | 2004
41½ X 52¼ INCHES (105.4 X 132.7 CM)
Cotton; hand appliquéd, machine quilted
PHOTO BY DAVID E. GLASOFER

Leslie Rego

Winter Interlude | 2006

44 X 27 INCHES (111.8 X 68.6 CM)

Cotton, metallic silk; hand dyed, machine embroidered, machine quilted

PHOTOS BY F. ALFREDO REGO

Molly Y. Hamilton-McNally
My Deer | 2005
40 X 40 INCHES (101.6 X 101.6 CM)
Cotton; appliquéd, hand quilted
PHOTO BY DAVID J. MCNALLY

Susan Shie

The Timer/Hanged One: Card #12 in the Kitchen Tarot | 2008

86 X 80 INCHES (218.4 X 203.2 CM)

Cotton, fabric paint, airbrush; machine quilted

PHOTO BY ARTIST

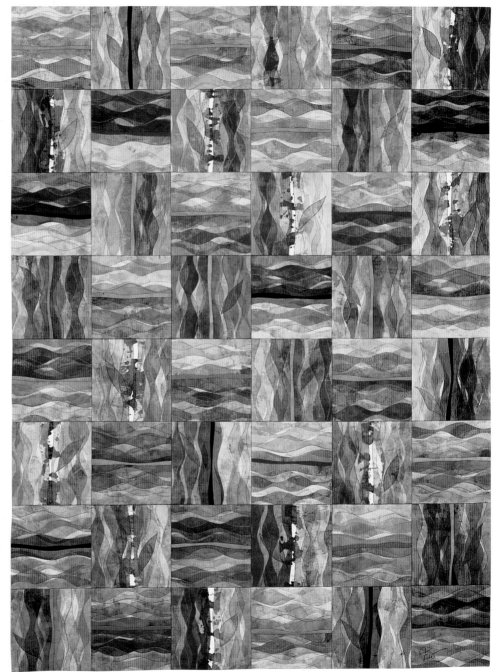

Nelda Warkentin
Autumn Splendor | 2003
68 X 51 INCHES (172.7 X 129.5 CM)
Silk, cotton, canvas, linen; painted
PHOTO BY JOHN TUCKEY

Linda Levin

Central Park West/Sunset | 2008

41 X 35 INCHES (104.1 X 88.9 CM)

Cotton, textile paint; machine stitched

PHOTOS BY JOE OFRIA

Nancy S. Brown
Elegy | 2008
22 X 27 INCHES (55.9 X 68.6 CM)
Cotton; hand appliquéd, hand quilted,
machine pieced
PHOTO BY ARTIST

Michele Heather Pollock
Monarch Migration | 2007
21 X 54 INCHES (53.3 X 137.2 CM)
Paper, cotton batting; machine quilted,
hand quilted
PHOTO BY ARTIST

Barbara Polston

Courage | 2008

28 X 28 INCHES (71.1 X 71.1 CM)

Cotton; painted, appliquéd, machine embroidered, machine quilted

PHOTOS BY ARTIST

Mary Goodson

Dipsea | 2005

36¹/₂ X 44 INCHES (91 .4 X 111.8 CM)

Cotton, dye, color pencil, fabric paint; discharged, shibori, pieced, appliquéd, machine quilted

PHOTO BY ARTIST

Noriko Endo

Radiant Reflections | 2008

66 X 80 INCHES (167.6 X 203.2 CM)

Cotton, luminescent fiber; machine appliquéd,
machine quilted, machine embroidered

PHOTO BY MASARU NOMURA

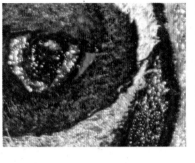

Ellen Anne Eddy

Hunter's Moon 2 | 2006

19 X 59 INCHES (48.3 X 149.9 CM)

Cotton, luminescent fiber, cheesecloth, brocade, organza, lace, polyester thread, metallic thread, nylon thread; hand dyed, embroidered, direct appliquéd, machine embroidered, machine quilted

PHOTOS BY ARTIST

Eileen Doughty

Root Domain | 2001

67 X 37 INCHES (170.2 X 94.0 CM)

Cotton, velvet, netting, ribbon, yarn, paint, ink, tree branch; machine pieced, appliquéd, quilted, thread drawn, collaged

PHOTO BY NEIL STEINBERG

Anita Kaplan

Imagine | 2008

59 X 53 INCHES (149.9 X 134.6 CM)

Cotton, cotton thread, silk thread; hand dyed, fused, painted, machine quilted

PHOTO BY MARK MCCUE

Elizabeth Barton

Where Bong Trees Grow | 2002

60 X 60 INCHES (152.4 X 152.4 CM)

Cotton; machine appliquéd, machine pieced, machine quilted, hand dyed, screen-printed, discharged

PHOTO BY ARTIST

Eileen Doughty

Below Great Falls | 2005

22 X 36 INCHES (55.9 X 91.4 CM)

Cotton, organza, acrylic paint, colored pencil;
machine pieced, appliquéd, quilted, thread drawn

PHOTOS BY ARTIST

Ludmila Aristova

Dusk | 2006

36 X 36 INCHES (91.4 X 91.4 CM)

Brocade, satin, taffeta, wool, tweed, cotton, silk, linen, viscose, netting, sequins; hand pieced, machine pieced, hand quilted, appliquéd

PHOTO BY KAREN BELL

Sandra van Velzen

Memory of Holland | 2008

62 X 52 INCHES (157.5 X 132.1 CM)

Cotton, thread, fiber, organza;
hand dyed, photo transferred,
painted, machine quilted

PHOTO BY ARTIST

Andrea Stewart

Moonlight and Shadows | 2008

54 X 86 INCHES (137.2 X 218.4 CM)

Cotton, water-soluble stabilizer, cotton batting; hand dyed, free-motion embroidered, machine quilted

PHOTOS BY ARTIST

Pat Kroth

Seasonal Shift | 2008

48 X 57 INCHES (121.9 X 144.7 CM)

Cotton, tulle overlays, silk, wool, other fibers;
hand dyed, machine stitched, heat-bond appliquéd

PHOTO BY ARTIST

Melody Randol

The Bench | 2006

30 X 72 INCHES (76.2 X 182.9 CM)

Cotton; hand painted, raw-edge appliquéd, machine quilted

PHOTO BY ARTIST

Wen Redmond

Kittery Point Marsh | 2008

EACH PANEL 27 X 12 INCHES
(68.6 X 30.5 CM)

Cotton sateen; collaged, printed, stitched

PHOTO BY ARTIST

Carol Watkins

Earth Poem | 2007

34 X 61 INCHES (86.4 X 154.9 CM)

Cotton, acrylic paint, synthetic fabrics; printed,
pieced, free-motion stitched, appliquéd

PHOTO BY KEN SANVILLE

Betty Busby

Refugee | 2008

72 X 62 INCHES (182.9 X 157.5 CM)

Cotton, batik, colored pencils; photo printed, over painted, burned, colored, raw-edge machine appliquéd, machine quilted

PHOTOS BY ALAN MITCHELL PHOTOGRAPHY

Sylvia Naylor

Fall in a Northern Wood | 2008

30 X 21¹/₂ INCHES (76.2 X 54.6 CM)

Polyester, organza, cotton, transfer dyes,
paint; free-motion machine embroidered

PHOTOS BY ARTIST

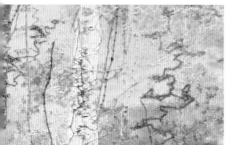

Patricia G. Faulkner
River Walk Swan | 2008
39 X 34 INCHES (99.1 X 86.4 CM)
Cotton; hand painted, hand
appliquéd, machine quilted
PHOTO BY TERRENCE W. FAULKNER

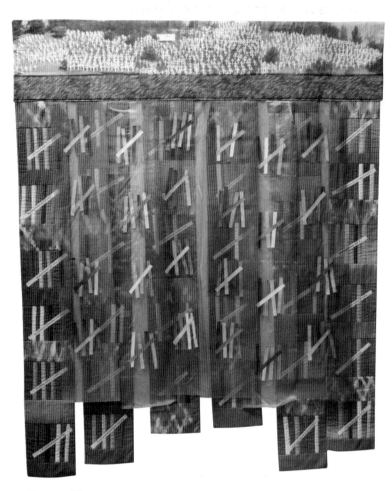

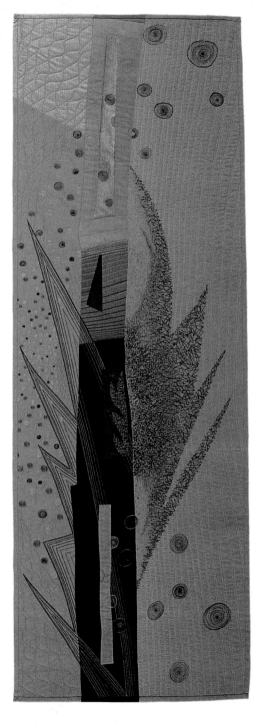

Karen Flamme

In Memoriam | 2007

64 X 53 INCHES (162.6 X 134.6 CM)

Cotton, silk organza, fusible web; hand dyed, photo transferred, machine pieced, fused, machine quilted

PHOTO BY ARTIST

Leslie C. Carabas

Salient | 2007

52 X 18 INCHES (132.1 X 45.7 CM)

Cotton, velvet; machine pieced, machine quilted

PHOTO BY ARTIST

Valerie C. White

Sun Goddess and the Blowing Leaves | 2006

20 X 16¹/₂ INCHES (50.8 X 41.9 CM)

Cotton/polyester fabric, disperse dyes; painted, hand embroidered, machine sewn

PHOTOS BY GEORGE PLAGER

Maggie Weiss

Iris | 2007

60 X 72 INCHES (152.4 X 182.9 CM)

Silk, cotton; hand dyed, fused,
hand cut, machine quilted

PHOTO BY PAUL LANE/PHOTO SOURCE

Rose Hughes

Riding the Thermals | 2008

45 X 45 INCHES (114.3 X 114.3 CM)

Silk, cotton, glass beads, wool beads, wool yarn, cotton embroidery floss; hand painted, hand dyed, appliquéd, machine quilted, machine couched, hand embroidered, hand beaded

PHOTO BY ARTIST

Kristin Tweed

#47 Big Head Series: The Story | 2006

43¹/₂ X 44¹/₂ INCHES (110.5 X 113.0 CM)

Cotton bedsheets, cotton thread, acrylic paint,
whole cloth; machine quilted

PHOTO BY ARTIST

Jo-Ann Golenia
Lucille | 2007
24¼ X 24¼ INCHES (61.6 X 61.6 CM)
Cotton, polyester trilobal thread,
fusible appliqué; machine quilted
PHOTO BY ARTIST

Susan Rienzo

A New Day: Sunshine Dreams and Memories | 2008

45 X 34 INCHES (114.3 X 86.4 CM)

Cotton; stitched, pieced, machine quilted

PHOTO BY ARTIST

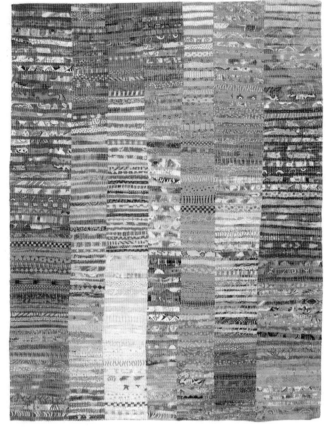

Jean M. Judd

Stained Glass Mosaic #2 | 2008

12³/₄ X 12³/₄ INCHES (32.4 X 32.4 CM)

Cotton, unbleached muslin; hand appliquéd, hand quilted, hand bound

PHOTO BY ARTIST

Ita Ziv

View to a Distance | 2008

47¹/₂ X 47¹/₂ INCHES (120.7 X 120.7 CM)

Scrim, cotton, metallic thread; hand dyed, machine pieced, machine quilted

PHOTO BY ARTIST

263

Anne McKenzie Nickolson

Who Will Lead Us? | 2006

46¹/₂ X 57 INCHES (118.1 X 144.8 CM)

Cotton; machine pieced, hand appliquéd

PHOTO BY ARTIST

Bonnie B. Ouellette

The Divine Miss M | 2008

14¹/₂ X 15 INCHES (36.8 X 38.1 CM)

Cotton, beads, sequins, charms;
hand quilted, hand embroidered

PHOTO BY ARTIST

Bodil Gardner

Heavenly Bodies | 2007

48 X 48 INCHES (121.9 X 121.9 CM)

Recycled fabrics, cotton; raw-edge machine appliquéd

PHOTO BY PETER GARDNER

Linda Barlow

One Day I'll Fly Away with the Birds and the Fishes | 2003

67 X 30 INCHES (170.2 X 76.2 CM)

Cotton; hand dyed, machine pieced, machine quilted, hand quilted

PHOTOS BY ARTIST

Debra Gabel
Batter | 2007
48 X 36 INCHES (121.9 X 91.4 CM)
Cotton, fabric paint, cord,
embellishments;
raw-edge appliquéd
PHOTO BY ARTIST

Bodil Gardner

Aunt Ada Remembers | 2008

34 X 40 INCHES (86.4 X 101.6 CM)

Recycled fabrics, cotton; raw-edge machine appliquéd

PHOTO BY PETER GARDNER

Stephanie Nordlin

Joyful Garden | 2008

18 X 20 (45.7 X 50.8 CM)

Cotton, thread, fusible appliqué;
decorative stitched, machine quilted

PHOTO BY ARTIST

Linda Gass

Fields of Salt | 2007

29¹/₂ X 29¹/₂ INCHES (74.9 X 74.9 CM)

Silk, paint; machine quilted

PHOTOS BY DON TUTTLE

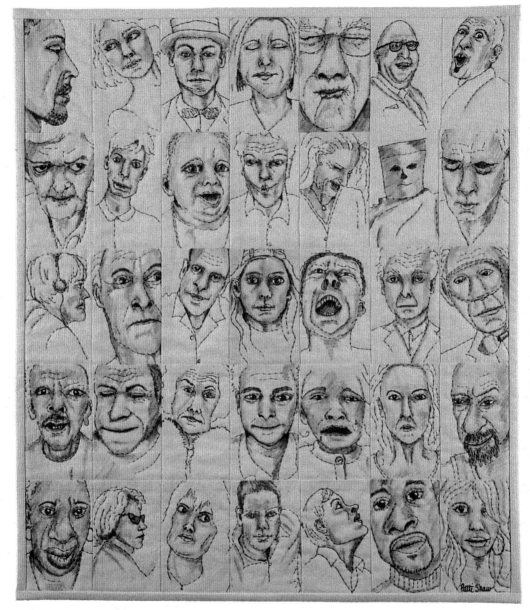

Patti Shaw

Thirty-Five | 2006

26$^{1/2}$ X 23$^{1/2}$ INCHES (67.3 X 59.7 CM)

Cotton, fabric pen; machine pieced, hand quilted

PHOTOS BY MARK FREY

Sandy Shelenberger
Gray Matter | 2008
45 X 36 INCHES (114.3 X 91.4 CM)
Cotton; machine pieced, free-motion machine quilted, airbrushed
PHOTO BY ARTIST

Dianne Firth
Cell Structure #7 | 2007
53 X 30 INCHES (134.6 X 76.2 CM)
Wool felt; reverse appliquéd, heat fused, machine quilted
PHOTO BY ANDREW SIKORSKI

Beth Porter Johnson
The Quilter | 2003
85 X 63 INCHES (215.9 X 160.0 CM)
Cotton; hand painted,
machine pieced, hand appliquéd,
machine quilted
PHOTOS BY MELLISA KARLIN MAHONEY

Susan Shie

The Potluck/World: Card #21 in the Kitchen Tarot | 2008

85 X 76 INCHES (215.9 X 193.0 CM)

Cotton, fabric paint, airbrush; machine quilted

PHOTOS BY ARTIST

Anne McKenzie Nickolson

Innocents | 2007

35 X 46 INCHES (88.9 X 116.8 CM)

Cotton; machine pieced, hand appliquéd

Teri McHale

Praise III | 2008

40 X 61½ INCHES
(101.6 X 156.2 CM)

Cotton, yarn; appliqué,
machine quilted,
couched

PHOTO BY ARTIST

Margot Lovinger

Surprise | 2006

21 X 35 INCHES (53.3 X 88.9 CM)

Cotton, silk, tulle,
netting; hand sewn,
hand embroidered,
hand beaded

PHOTO BY ARTIST

Kristin Tweed

#11 The Big Head Series: The Bar | 2002

46 X 45 1/2 INCHES (116.8 X 115.6 CM)

Cotton bedsheets, cotton thread, acrylic paint,
whole cloth; machine quilted

PHOTO BY ARTIST

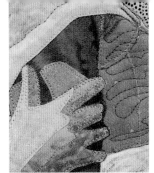

Joan Sowada
Nicely Grounded | 2007
15¹/₂ X 21 INCHES (39.4 X 53.3 CM)
Cotton, oil pastel sticks; fused,
machine appliquéd, machine quilted
PHOTOS BY DAVID NICHOLAS

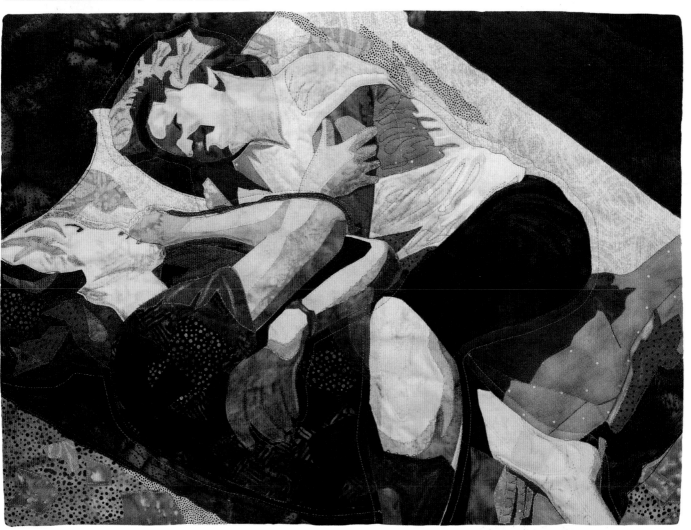

Kathleen McCabe

In His Shadow | 2008

29 X 33 INCHES (73.7 X 83.8 CM)

Cotton, nylon tulle; machine appliquéd, machine quilted

PHOTO BY PHIL IMMING

Alice Beasley

Global Warning | 2006

26 X 24 INCHES (66.0 X 61.0 CM)

Cotton; machine appliquéd, machine quilted

PHOTO BY DON TUTTLE

Deborah K. Snider

Color Wheel: Stereotypes | 2006

50 X 42 INCHES (127.0 X 106.7 CM)

Cotton, beads; raw-edge appliquéd,
free-motion machine quilted

PHOTO BY HAROLD D. SNIDER

Kim Ritter

Handy Woman Tools | 2004

32 X 24 INCHES (81.3 X 61.0 CM)

Silk; printed, stamped, machine pieced, quilted

PHOTO BY ARTIST

Linda Rudin Frizzell

Mandala | 2006

28 X 28 INCHES (71.1 X 71.1 CM)

Cotton; machine appliquéd, machine quilted

PHOTO BY MARK FREY

Cody Marie Mazuran

Allsorts | 2007

54 X 45 INCHES (137.2 X 114.3 CM)

Cotton; machine pieced, machine appliquéd, machine quilted, embellished

PHOTO BY KENT SHELTON

B.J. Reed

Horsepower: Red Mustang | 2006

30 X 38 INCHES (76.2 X 96.5 CM)

Prints; disperse dyed, hand quilted,
free-motion machine quilted

PHOTO BY ARTIST

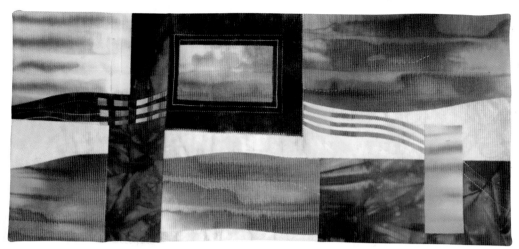

Karen Flamme
Sunrise, Sunset | 2007
10 X 23 INCHES (25.4 X 58.4 CM)
Cotton, silk; hand dyed,
fused, hand quilted,
machine quilted
PHOTO BY ARTIST

Laura Wasilowski
Housing Department #17 | 2008
12 X 15 INCHES (30.5 X 38.1 CM)
Cotton, interfacing; appliquéd,
hand embroidered, machine quilted
PHOTO BY ARTIST

Elsie Vredenburg
Fresh Snow | 2006
58 X 41 INCHES (147.3 X 104.1 CM)
Cotton; hand dyed, machine
pieced, machine quilted,
machine embroidered
PHOTO BY ARTIST

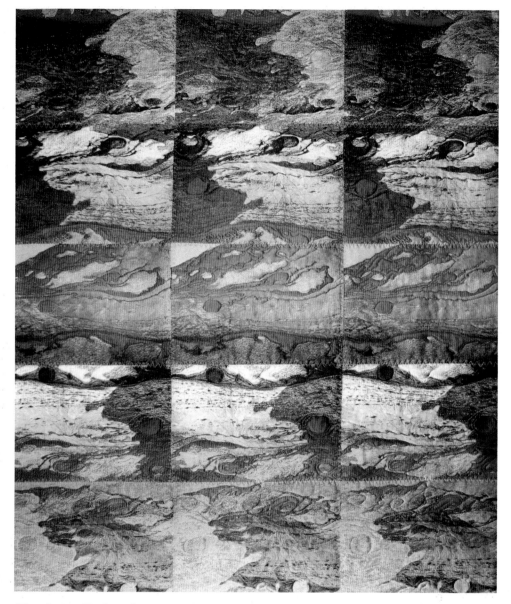

Charlotte Ziebarth

Moon and Mars: Sand Pictures #3 | *2007*

42 X 34 INCHES (106.6 X 86.3 CM)

Silk, pigment inks, digitally altered photos;
fused appliqué, free-motion machine quilted

PHOTO BY ARTIST

Linda Hall

Falling Leaves | 2007

48 X 34 INCHES (121.9 X 86.3 CM)

Cotton, polyester, flannel,
upholstery fabric, mohair yarn,
merino wool roving, silk,
metallic threads, copper sheet,
metal wire; machine quilted,
needle felted, free-motion
embroidered, hammered

PHOTO BY ARTIST

Valerie Hearder

Life Line: Displacement | 2000

36 X 39 INCHES (91.4 X 99.1 CM)

Silk, taffeta, cotton, metallic mesh; appliquéd,
machine pieced, machine quilted

PHOTO BY BRIAN RICKS

Kathy McNeil

Take Me There | 2008

63 1/2 X 50 INCHES (161.3 X 127.0 CM)

Cotton, silk organza, tulle, yarn; hand appliquéd, machine quilted

PHOTOS BY BRUCE MCNEIL

Melody Randol

Fifty Years | 2007

36 X 50 INCHES (91.4 X 127.0 CM)

Cotton; hand dyed, painted, discharged, raw-edge appliquéd, machine quilted

PHOTOS BY ARTIST

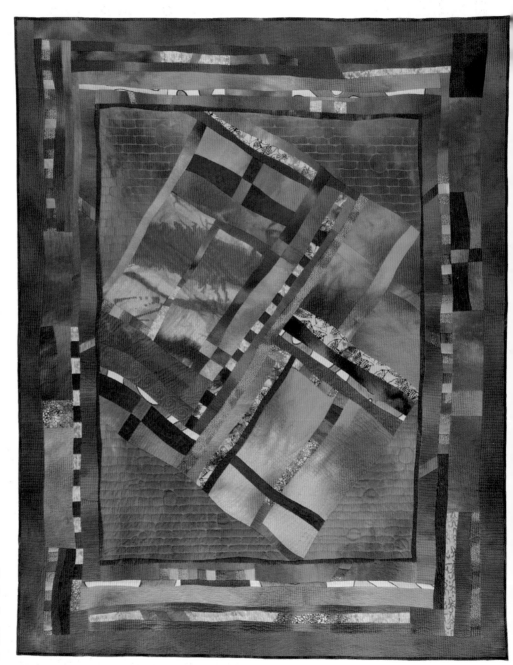

Barbara Oliver Hartman

Reclamation: Retro | 2008

82 X 66 INCHES (208.3 X 167.6 CM)

Cotton, silk, rayon; pieced,
machine quilted

PHOTO BY ERIC NEILSON

Ellen Lindner

Out of the Blue | 2006

20½ X 13½ INCHES (52.1 X 34.3 CM)

Cotton, silk; hand painted,
raw-edge collaged, machine quilted

PHOTO BY ARTIST

Caryl Bryer Fallert

Feather Study #30 | 2007

65 X 53 INCHES (165.1 X 134.6 CM)

Cotton, cotton/polyester batting,
polyester thread; hand dyed, hand painted,
machine pieced, machine quilted

PHOTO BY ARTIST

Jill Jensen
Cactus Flower | 2008
25¹/₂ X 25 INCHES (64.8 X 63.5 CM)
Canvas, paint, colored pencil;
hand painted, hand quilted
PHOTO BY ARTIST

Elaine Quehl
Opening Act | 2007
39 X 48 INCHES (121.9 X 78.7 CM)
Fabric, fusible appliqué, wax pastels,
crayons; hand dyed, machine quilted
PHOTO BY ARTIST

Juanita G. Yeager
Poppies on Checkered Ground | 2007
28 X 54 INCHES (71.1 X 137.2 CM)
Cotton, rice paste, dye, fabric markers; painted,
machine quilted, thread worked
PHOTO BY ARTIST

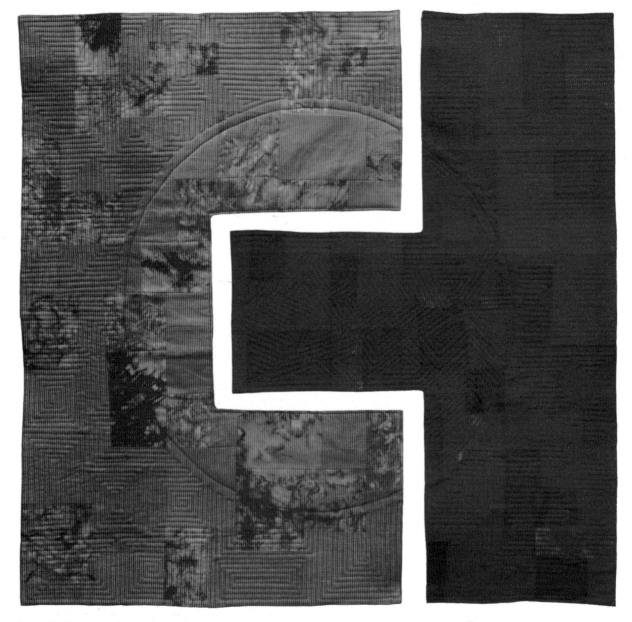

Laurie Brainerd

Now (Diptych) | 2008

29¹/₂ X 30³/₄ INCHES (74.9 X 78.1 CM)

Cotton, recycled garments; machine pieced, machine quilted

PHOTO BY ARTIST

Ineke van Unen

Silk Route | 2007

32 X 24 INCHES (81.3 X 61.0 CM)

Commercial fabric, cotton, plastic, polyester, metallic thread; hand dyed, machine appliquéd, machine quilted, machine embroidered

PHOTO BY F.R. VAN UNEN

Andrea L. Stern
Marilyn | 2008
62 X 76 INCHES (157.5 X 193.0 CM)
Cotton, beads, sequins; machine pieced, machine
appliquéd, machine quilted, hand embellished
PHOTO BY MARTY STERN

Clare Smith

I'd Rather See Windmills | 2006

53 X 41 INCHES (134.6 X 104.1 CM)

Cotton; hand painted, screen-printed,
raw-edge appliquéd, machine quilted

Stephanie Nordlin

P Cubed (Prime. Primary. Primordial) | 2008

42¼ X 42¾ INCHES (107.3 X 108.6 CM)

Cotton, beads, sequins; machine appliquéd,
machine quilted, hand beaded

Ree Nancarrow

Polychrome | 2007

36½ X 37½ INCHES (92.7 X 95.3 CM)

Cotton; stenciled, dye painted, stamped, silk-screened, machine pieced, machine quilted

PHOTO BY ARTIST

Grietje van der Veen

Lavaux | 2008

32 X 58 INCHES (81.3 X 147.3 CM)

Cotton, felt, fabric, yarn, cord, acrylic paint; hand dyed, layered, hand embroidered, machine quilted

PHOTOS BY KUNO MATHIS

Sue Holdaway-Heys

The Arb House | 2008

61 X 50 INCHES (154.9 X 127.0 CM)

Cotton; hand painted, dyed, fused, machine quilted

PHOTO BY ARTIST

Jen Swearington

Tideland | 2008

44 X 42 INCHES (111.8 X 106.7 CM)

Bedsheets, silk, gesso, shellac, ink, charcoal; machine pieced, machine quilted

PHOTO BY ARTIST

Candy Flynn

Edge of the World | 2005

35 X 35 INCHES (88.9 X 88.9 CM)

Commercial-cotton batik; machine pieced, hand quilted

PHOTO BY JOHN KABOT

Jan Myers-Newbury

Wild Thing . . . | 2008

60 X 80 INCHES (152.4 X 203.2 CM)

Cotton; shibori, machine pieced, machine quilted

PHOTO BY SAM NEWBERRY

Carol Cassidy

On the Edge | 2005

40 X 50 INCHES (101.6 X 127.0 CM)

Cotton; machine appliquéd, machine quilted

PHOTOS BY ARTIST

Barbara W. Watler

Autumn | 2007

107 X 240 INCHES (271.8 X 609.6 CM)

Cotton, batting; hand dyed, reversed appliquéd, machine stitched, machine embellished

PHOTOS BY GERHARD HEIDERSBERGER

Carol Watkins

Woodland Memory III | 2008

33 X 30 INCHES (83.8 X 76.2 CM)

Cotton, acrylic paint, digitally manipulated photographs;
hand dyed, printed, pieced, appliquéd, free-motion stitched

PHOTO BY KEN SANVILLE

Kathy McNeil

Walk with Me | 2006

76¹/₂ X 46¹/₂ INCHES (194.3 X 118.1 CM)

Tulle, yarn; sculpted, hand appliquéd,
machine appliquéd, hand dyed

PHOTO BY BRUCE MCNEIL

Larkin Jean Van Horn

Gaia | 2007

45 X 18 INCHES (114.3 X 45.7 CM)

Cotton, commercial batik, beads,
sequins; hand dyed, fused, machine
appliquéd, machine quilted, hand beaded

PHOTO BY G. ARMOUR VAN HORN

Pamela Zave
Sunlight, Citron, Saffron, Ochre | 2006
43 X 56 INCHES (109.2 X 142.2 CM)
Cotton; machine pieced, machine quilted
PHOTO BY YOLANDA V. FUNDORA

Diana F. Sharkey
Cat under the Sun | 2007

100 X 80 INCHES (254.0 X 203.2 CM)

Cotton; pieced, machine quilted

MACHINE QUILTED BY WILMA COGLIANTRY
PHOTOS BY WILLIAM LULOW

Marie Jensen
Blink | 2005
24 X 34 INCHES (61.0 X 86.4 CM)
Cotton; painted, machine pieced, machine quilted
PHOTO BY KEVIN MCGOWAN

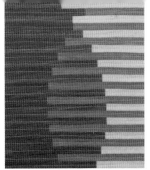

Kent Williams

Sine Me Up | 2008

90 X 60 INCHES (228.6 X 152.4 CM)

Cotton; machine pieced, machine quilted

PHOTOS BY ERIC TADSEN

Odette Tolksdorf

Broken Bones and Ladders | 1998

31 X 31 INCHES (78.7 X 78.7 CM)

Cotton; hand dyed, machine pieced,
hand quilted

PHOTO BY ARTIST

Susan Krueger

On Phrenology | 2000

38 X 27 INCHES (96.5 X 68.6 CM)

Cotton, plastic charms, beads,
sequins; hand embroidered,
hand quilted, machine quilted

PHOTOS BY LOU KRUEGER

Pixeladies—Deb Cashatt and Kris Sazaki

Just(ice) in Time? | 2008

40 X 30 INCHES (101.6 X 76.2 CM)

Cotton; custom printed, hand quilted

Ginny Eckley
Hospital Rising | 2008
41 X 41 INCHES (104.1 X 104.1 CM)
Silk; silk-screened, painted, dyed
PHOTO BY ARTIST

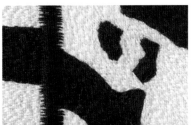

Barbara W. Watler

Fingerprint Series #46: Vortex | 2006

54 X 54 INCHES (137.2 X 137.2 CM)

Canvas, cotton; thread painted, machine stitched

PHOTOS BY GERHARD HEIDERSBERGER

Beth P. Gilbert

The Underground Railroad | 2006

53 X 51¼ INCHES (134.6 X 51.25 CM)

Cotton; machine pieced, machine appliquéd, fused, photo transferred, painted, inked, machine embroidered, machine quilted

PHOTOS BY ARTIST

Mary Elmusa

Insight | 2008

27 X 20 INCHES (68.6 X 50.8 CM)

Cotton, interfacing; painted, printed, machine quilted

PHOTOS BY ARTIST

Marlene Ferrell Parillo

Stages of Grief | 2008

50 X 45 INCHES (127.0 X 114.3 CM)

Cotton, beads, clay, refractory wire; hand embroidered, sewn

PHOTOS BY HOWARD GOODMAN

Nancy Crasco

Phaeophyta | 2006

60 X 60 INCHES (152.4 X 152.4 CM)

Silk organza, mulberry paper; machine pieced, hand quilted, machine quilted

PHOTOS BY STEVE GYURINA

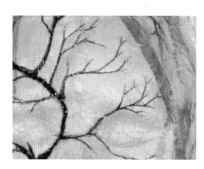

Christina Brown

In the Forest of You | 2005

21¾ X 21¾ INCHES (55.2 X 56.5 CM)

Cotton, silk paper; machine quilted, hand embroidered, painted

PHOTOS BY ARTIST

Noriko Endo

Autumn Enchantment | 2008

89 X 67 INCHES (226.1 X 170.2 CM)

Cotton, luminescent fiber, paint; machine appliquéd, machine quilted, machine embroidered

PHOTO BY MASARU NOMURA

Terry Waldron

Hey Kahuna! No Trespassing! | 2008
40 X 56 INCHES (101.6 X 142.2 CM)

Cotton, polyester, glass beads, stones, cotton thread;
overdyed, woven, hand appliquéd, fused, machine
quilted, hand beaded

PHOTOS BY ARTIST

Anita Kaplan
Kelp | 204
42 X 31 INCHES (106.7 X 78.7 CM)
Cotton; hand dyed, machine
appliquéd, machine quilted
PHOTO BY MARK MCCUE

Ginny Eckley
Koi Under the Willow | 2006
26 X 21 INCHES (66.0 X 53.3 CM)
Silk; inkjet printed, free-motion embroidered,
hand painted
PHOTOS BY RICK WELLS

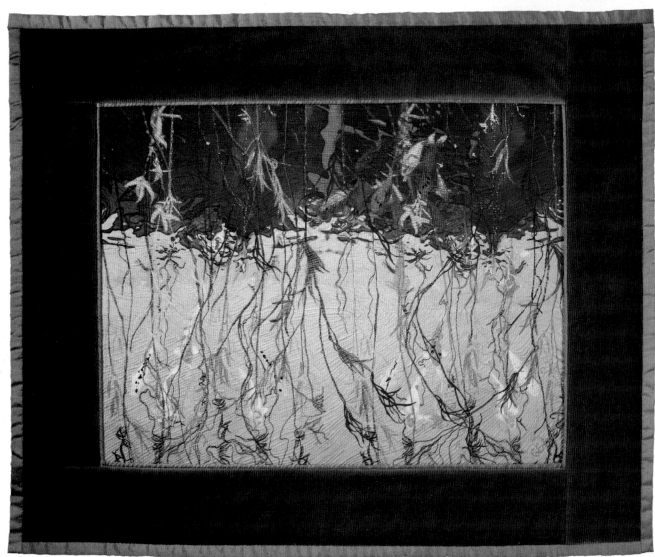

Nancy G. Cook

Spring Rhapsody | 2008

36 X 27 INCHES (91.4 X 68.6 CM)

Cotton sateen; machine quilted, inked, hand embroidered

PHOTOS BY MITCHELL KEARNEY

Julia E. Pfaff

My Summer in Tragana | 2006

31 X 31 INCHES (78.7 X 78.7 CM)

Cotton, cotton embroidery floss; dye printed, hand embroidered, machine pieced, free-motion quilted

PHOTO BY TAYLOR DABNEY

Tommy Fitzsimmons
Falling Down #3 | 2006
54¹⁄₂ X 53 INCHES (138.4 X 134.6 CM)
Cotton; hand dyed, machine pieced,
machine quilted
PHOTO BY ARTIST

Leslie A. Hall
Phobos Kenesis | 2007
67 X 67 INCHES (170.2 X 170.2 CM)
Cotton; hand dyed, machine pieced,
machine quilted, hand embroidered
PHOTOS BY PHILIP W. HALL

Nancy S. Brown

Sunday in the Park with Mittens | 2005

47 X 58 INCHES (119.4 X 147.3 CM)

Cotton; hand appliquéd, hand quilted, machine pieced

PHOTO BY ARTIST

Nancy S. Brown

The Usual Suspects | 2006

45 X 45½ INCHES (114.3 X 115.6 CM)

Cotton; hand appliquéd, hand quilted, machine pieced

PHOTO BY ARTIST

Gloria Hansen

Squared Illusions 6 | 2007

44 X 34 INCHES (111.8 X 86.4 CM)

Silk, cotton, fabric paint; machine
pieced, machine quilted

PHOTO BY ARTIST

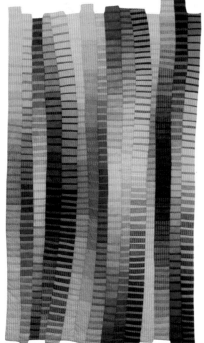

Anne R. Parker

Gradations | 2008

72 X 42 INCHES (182.9 X 106.7 CM)

Cotton; hand dyed, machine pieced, hand quilted

PHOTO BY ARTIST

Dan Olfe

Cylinder Reflections #2 | 2008

52 X 51 INCHES (132.1 X 129.5 CM)

Polyester; digitally printed

PHOTO BY ARTIST

Wendy Butler Berns

Pure Joy . . . Imagine That! | 2006

51 X 51 INCHES (129.5 X 129.5 CM)

Cotton, specialty threads; machine appliquéd,
machine quilted

PHOTO BY ARTIST

Caryl Bryer Fallert

On the Wings of a Dream | 2008

64 X 63 INCHES (162.6 X 160.0 CM)

Cotton, cotton/polyester batting, polyester thread;
hand dyed, hand painted, machine pieced, machine quilted

PHOTOS BY ARTIST

Jennifer A. Wheatley-Wolf

Approaching Winter | 2006

51 X 66 INCHES (129.5 X 167.6 CM)

Silk, cotton prints, satin, beads, upholstery corduroy, upholstery tweed; appliquéd, thread painted, machine embroidered, free-style quilted

PHOTO BY ARTIST

Ruth Powers

Bittersweet Memories | 2005

62½ X 49½ INCHES (158.8 X 125.7 CM)

Cotton, crystal; machine pieced, machine quilted

PHOTOS BY ARTIST

Nancy B. Dickey

Windswept | 2003

55 X 55 INCHES (139.7 X 139.7 CM)

Cotton; machine appliquéd, machine quilted, machine trapunto

PHOTOS BY MIKE MCCORMICK

Maggie Weiss

Canopy | 2007

52 X 48 INCHES (132.1 X 121.9 CM)

Silk, cotton; hand dyed, fused, hand cut, collaged, machine quilted

PHOTO BY PAUL LANE/PHOTO SOURCE

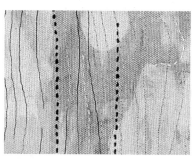

Clairan Ferrono

Last Conversation | 2007

19 X 21 INCHES (48.3 X 53.3 CM)

Cotton, canvas; hand painted,
hand stitched, machine quilted

PHOTOS BY TOM VAN EYNDE

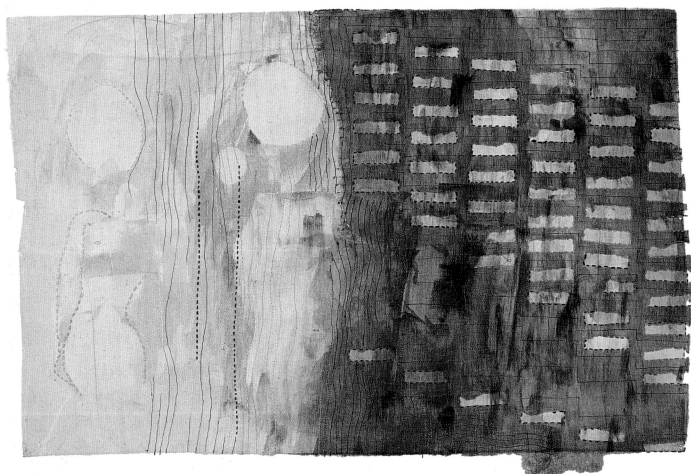

Eszter Bornemisza

New Icon Wall | 2007

56 X 36 INCHES (142.2 X 91.4 CM)

Cotton, tulle, synthetic organza; dyed, burned, silk-screened, hot cut, machine appliquéd, machine quilted

PHOTO BY TIHANYI-BAKOS

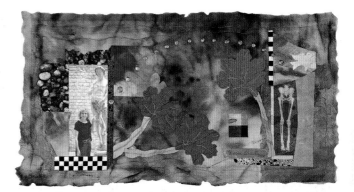

Yvonne Porcella

Paris View, Lou & Who, Two & Two | 2008

40 X 25 INCHES (101.6 X 63.5 CM)

Cotton, silk, acrylic, paper, iridescent ink, foil, fabric paint, colored pencil; photo transferred, fused, machine stitched, hand stitched, burned, colored

PHOTO BY DAVID LUTZ

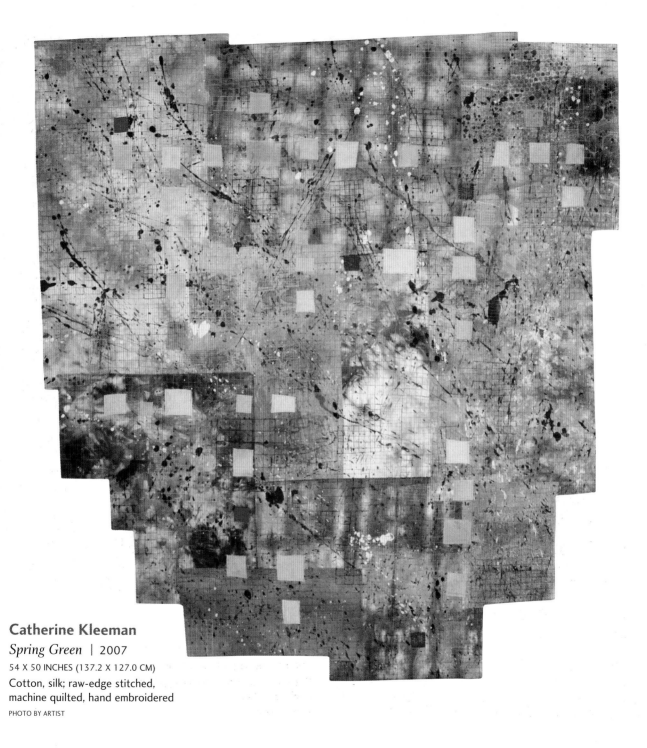

Catherine Kleeman
Spring Green | 2007
54 X 50 INCHES (137.2 X 127.0 CM)
Cotton, silk; raw-edge stitched,
machine quilted, hand embroidered
PHOTO BY ARTIST

Sherry D. Shine
Pray for Peace | 2008
28 X 24 INCHES (53.3 X 61.0 CM)
Acrylic, cotton; appliquéd, machine quilted
PHOTO BY MARCUS SHINE

Colleen Ansbaugh
Portrait: Dan the Man | 2008
41¹/₂ X 32 INCHES (105.4 X 81.3 CM)
Cotton; hand dyed, machine appliquéd,
machine quilted
PHOTO BY ARTIST

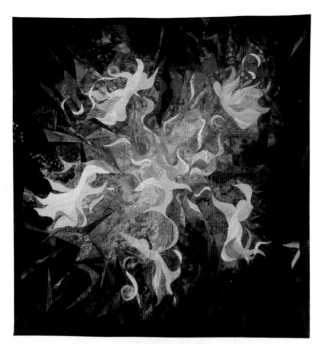

Vikki Pignatelli
Passages of the Spirit | 2002
72¼ X 69 INCHES (183.4 X 175.3 CM)
Cotton, metallic lamé; appliquéd,
pieced, free-motion machine quilted
PHOTO BY ARTIST

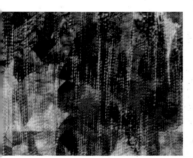

Ludmila Aristova
Summer Rain | 2005
28 X 40 INCHES (71.1 X 101.6 CM)
Cotton, silk; machine pieced,
machine quilted
PHOTOS BY D. JAMES DEE

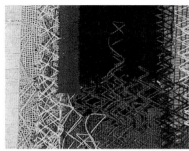

Sarah Symes

Joy | 2007

31 X 24 INCHES (78.7 X 61.0 CM)

Cotton, silk, velvet; machine appliquéd,
machine embroidered

PHOTOS BY ADAM REDNER

Esterita Austin

Sunday Morning | 2006

59 X 54 INCHES (149.9 X 137.2 CM)

Cotton, silk, lace, tulle, velvet; fused, painted,
machine quilted

PHOTO BY ARTIST

Marilyn H. Wall

Peacockiness | 2007

41 X 41 INCHES (104.1 X 104.1 CM)

Cotton, paint; hand dyed, machine appliquéd, machine quilted

MACHINE QUILTED BY DIANA PICKENS
PHOTO BY KERMIT WALL

Sue Holdaway-Heys
Passage | 2007
58 X 47 INCHES (147.3 X 119.4 CM)
Cotton; hand painted, fused, machine quilted

Holly Knott
New Hope, PA, Reflections 1 | 2003
28 X 18 INCHES (71.1 X 45.7 CM)
Cotton, textile paint; machine appliquéd,
machine quilted

Vikki Pignatelli

The Promise of Spring | 2005

73 X 62 INCHES (185.4 X 157.5 CM)

Cotton, metallic lamé, sheers,
organza, beads; appliquéd, pieced,
free-motion quilted

PHOTO BY ARTIST

Elaine Quehl

Standing Still | 2008

29 X 21 INCHES (53.3 X 73.7 CM)

Fabric, fusible appliqué; hand dyed, free-hand
pieced, thread painted, machine quilted

PHOTO BY ARTIST

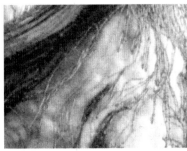

Jayne Bentley Gaskins

Ancient Roots | 2008

22 X 32 INCHES (55.9 X 81.3 CM)

Cotton, semi-transparent material; thread painted, machine appliquéd, machine quilted, trapunto, photo transferred

PHOTOS BY ARTIST

Alessandra Billingslea
My "Let It Be" Place | 2006
33 X 29 INCHES (83.8 X 73.7)
Cotton, fiber, beads, thread; machine embroidered
PHOTO BY ARTIST

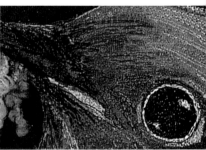

Nancy Murty

Greens for Dinner | 2004

25 X 39 INCHES (63.5 X 99.1 CM)

Cotton, silk; hand painted, machine stitched

PHOTOS BY ANDREW GILLIS

351

Robin M. Haller
The Cache | 1997

51 X 41 INCHES (129.5 X 104.1 CM)

Cotton; machine appliquéd,
machine pieced, fused, machine
quilted, machine embroidered

PHOTO BY ARTIST

Pat Owoc

Urban Evening | 2006

51 X 50 INCHES (129.5 X 127.0 CM)

Polyester; disperse dyed, machine quilted

PHOTO BY CASEY RAE (RED ELF, INC.)

Linda Barlow

She Was Riding a Bear | 2005

57 X 40 INCHES (144.8 X 101.6 CM)

Cotton, linen, silk organdy, polyester organdy; hand dyed, painted, pieced, appliquéd, machine quilted

PHOTOS BY ARTIST

Louisa L. Smith

Changing Gears | 2005

41¹/₂ X 50 INCHES (105.4 X 127.0 CM)

Commercial cotton, fabric, paper; machine pieced, machine appliquéd, machine quilted

PHOTO BY ARTIST

Deidre Adams

Composition VIII | 2008

39 X 39 INCHES (99.1 X 99.1 CM)

Cotton fabric, acrylic paint; machine quilted, hand painted

PHOTO BY ARTIST

Hilary Gooding
*There's Some Corner
of a Foreign Field . . .* | 2008
29 X 39½ INCHES (73.7 X 100.3 CM)
Cotton; machine pieced, hand appliquéd,
machine embroidered, painted,
machine quilted
PHOTO BY ARTIST

Sandy Gregg
Swirl 6 | 2007
36 X 35 INCHES (91.4 X 88.9 CM)
Cotton, silk, fabric; hand dyed, hand
painted, machine quilted
PHOTO BY ARTIST

Anna Hergert

Navigating the Canadian Shield: Bedrock and Trees | 2008

44 X 42 INCHES (111.7 X 106.6 CM)

Cotton, oil sticks; hand dyed, appliquéd, machine quilted

PHOTO BY ARTIST

Annette Morgan
Serendipity | 2005
36 X 36 INCHES (91.4 X 91.4 CM)
Cotton, synthetic fabric, soldering iron;
dyed, quilted, burned, cut
PHOTOS BY KEVIN MEAD

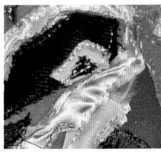

Laura Fogg

A Dark Angel's Plea for the Salvation of Our Planet | 2007

80 X 60 INCHES (203.2 X 152.4 CM)

Cotton, silk, satin, tulle, novelty trims, photographs; machine pieced, machine appliquéd, machine quilted, digitally printed

PHOTOS BY ARTIST

Deborah Sylvester

Life Reflections | 2007

40 X 41 INCHES (101.6 X 104.1 CM)

Cotton; machine pieced, appliquéd, machine quilted

Elizabeth Poole

Study in Aubergines | 2007

12 X 9 INCHES (30.5 X 22.9 CM)

Cotton; machine appliquéd, machine quilted

Pamela Allen

Lady Luck | 2005

37 X 27 INCHES (94.0 X 68.6 CM)

Recycled fabric, commercial silk and rayon, found objects; hand appliquéd, machine quilted, embellished

PHOTO BY ARTIST

Shin-hee Chin

Esubalew | 2008

49 X 38 INCHES (124.5 X 96.5 CM)

Cotton, mixed and recycled fabrics; hand stitched

PHOTOS BY JIM TURNER

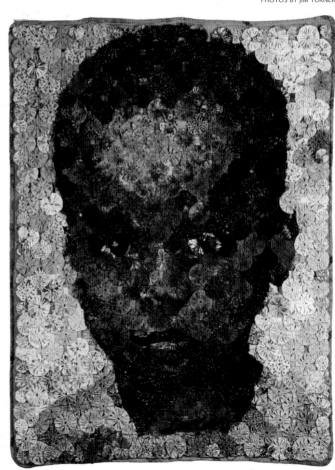

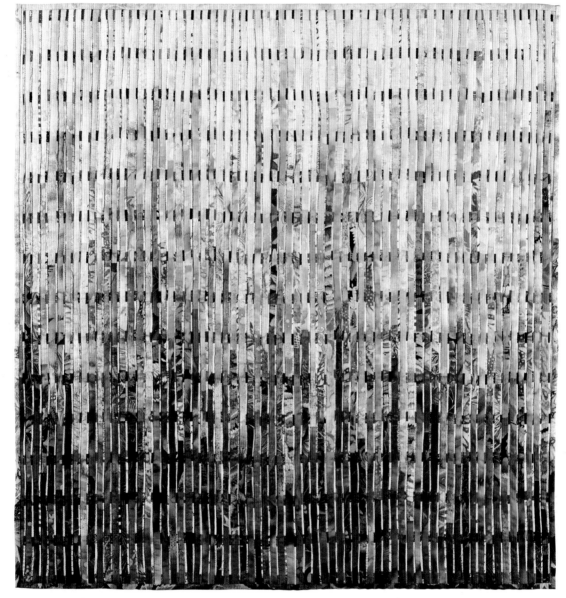

Margery Goodall

Liquid Amber | 2004

27½ X 27½ INCHES (69.9 X 69.9 CM)

Cotton, silk, rayon, ink; machine stitched

PHOTOS BY ADRIAN LAMBERT/ACORN PHOTO AGENCY

Jeannie Palmer Moore

Roundabout Reds | 2008

40 X 37¹/₂ INCHES (101.6 X 95.3 CM)

Cotton, silk, organza, cheesecloth,
fabric paints; hand dyed, stamped, printed,
discharged, machine appliquéd

PHOTOS BY BOB HILL/PHOTO DARKROOM

Mindy Fitterman

Out on a Limb | 2008

20³/₄ X 20³/₄ INCHES (52.7 X 52.7 CM)

Cotton; machine pieced

PHOTO BY ARTIST

Melody Randol

Grandeur and Granite | 2006

39 X 64 INCHES (99.1 X 162.6 CM)

Cotton, sheers, burlap strands, yarn; hand dyed, thread painted, machine quilted, raw-edge appliquéd

PHOTO BY ARTIST

Marla Hattabaugh

Family Is Growing | 2005

38 X 74 INCHES (96.5 X 188.0 CM)

Cotton; hand processed, machine pieced, hand quilted

PHOTO BY ARTIST

Beth Miller

Bush Larrikins | 2003

72½ X 62 INCHES (184.2 X 162.2 CM)

Cotton; hand painted, appliquéd, machine quilted

PHOTO BY DAVID PATERSON

Carol Taylor

Dispersion | 2005

75 1/2 X 68 1/2 INCHES (191.8 X 174 CM)

Cotton sateen, yarn; hand dyed, appliquéd, stitched, couched

PHOTO BY ARTIST

Judith Content

Prism | 2007

91 X 53 INCHES (231.1 X 134.6 CM)

Silk charmeuse; shibori, pieced, discharged, machine quilted

PHOTO BY JAMES DEWRANCE

Marie Jensen

The Day the Sky Fell Down | 2003

40 X 28 INCHES (101.6 X 71.1 CM)

Cotton, paper, fusible appliqué; painted, machine quilted

PHOTO BY KEVIN MCGOWAN

Patti Shaw

Picture Day | 2006

21³/₄ X 26¹/₂ INCHES (55.2 X 67.3 CM)

Cotton, fabric pen, paint; machine pieced, hand quilted

PHOTO BY MARK FREY

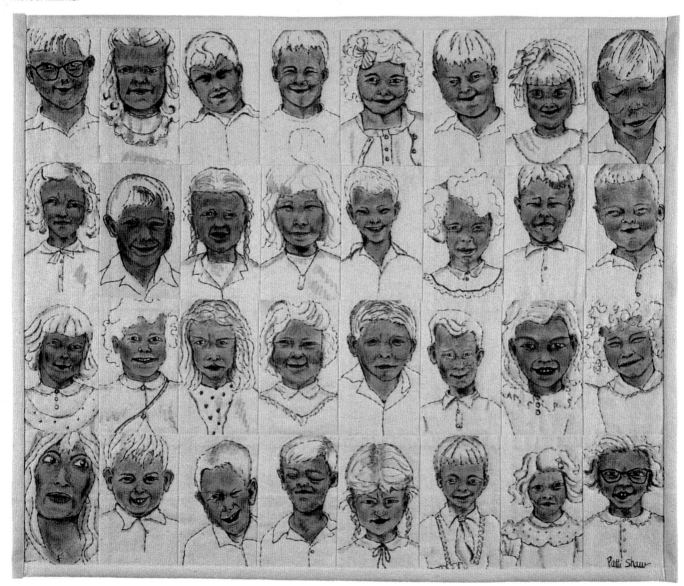

Sandra Hoefner
Flying Saucers | 1999
68 X 47 INCHES (172.7 X 119.4 CM)
Cotton, piping; hand
appliquéd, quilted
PHOTOS BY VICTOR C. HOEFNER III

Natasha Kempers-Cullen

Stephanie's Quilt | 2001

70 X 51 INCHES (177.8 X 129.5 CM)

Cotton, tulle, fiber-reactive dye, textile paint, metallic thread, rayon thread, glass seed beads, glass leaf beads, charms; painted, printed, collaged, machine quilted, hand beaded

PHOTOS BY DENNIS GRIGGS

Elaine Quehl

Soleil II | 2006

59 X 45 INCHES (149.8 X 114.3 CM)

Commercial batiks, ink, fabric; hand dyed, pieced, raw-edge appliquéd, machine quilted

PHOTO BY ARTIST

Alice Beasley
The Basket Maker | 2008
43 X 49 INCHES (109.2 X 124.5 CM)
Cotton; machine appliquéd, machine quilted

Suanne Reed
Thalia | 2008
22 X 30 INCHES (55.9 X 76.2 CM)
Fabric, wool roving, novelty yarn; hand
dyed, appliquéd, machine quilted
PHOTOS BY ARTIST

Margo Fiddes
Grape Hyacinth | 2007
27 X 60 INCHES (68.6 X 152.4 CM)
Cotton; machine pieced,
machine quilted
PHOTO BY VINCENT WALDON

Beth Porter Johnson
Tree Talk | 2008
24³/₄ X 38 INCHES (62.9 X 96.5 CM)
Cotton; machine appliquéd,
machine quilted
PHOTO BY ARTIST

Joan Sowada

Pink | 2007

39 X 38 INCHES (99.1 X 96.5 CM)

Cotton, oil pastel sticks, silk thread; hand dyed,
fused, machine appliquéd, machine quilted

PHOTO BY DAVID NICHOLAS

Margo Fiddes

Apple Blossoms | 2006

38 X 30 INCHES (96.5 X 76.2 CM)

Cotton; machine pieced,
machine quilted

PHOTO BY VINCENT WALDON

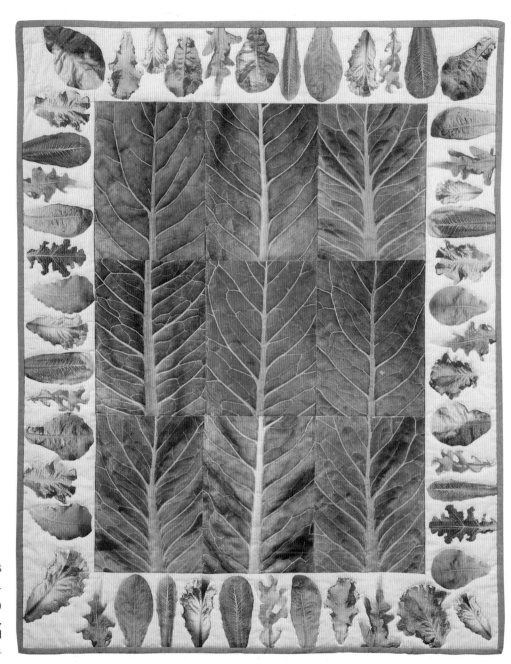

Elia Woods

Salad Ballad | 2004

35 X 28 INCHES (88.9 X 71.1 CM)

Cotton; photo transferred,
machine pieced, machine quilted

PHOTO BY KEITH BALL

Lori Lupe Pelish

The Gift | 2006

52 X 32 INCHES (132.1 X 81.3 CM)

Cotton; machine appliquéd, machine quilted, machine embroidered, knotted

PHOTO BY DAVID PELISH

Nancy Murty

Love, Honor, and Cherish | 2004

86 X 39 INCHES (218.4 X 99.1 CM)

Cotton, silk; hand painted, silk-screened, machine appliquéd, machine quilted

PHOTO BY ANDREW GILLIS

Julie Duschack

Moth Fairy | 2003

60 X 70 INCHES (152.4 X 177.8 CM)

Cotton, tulle, upholstery fabric; reverse machine appliquéd, thread painted

PHOTOS BY ARTIST

Toni Kersey

Urban Voodoo (2) | 2008

55 X 42 INCHES (139.7 X 106.7 CM)

Cotton, silk, commercial fabric, buttons; photo transferred, printed, raw-edge appliquéd, machine pieced, machine quilted

PHOTO BY LEE MOSKOW

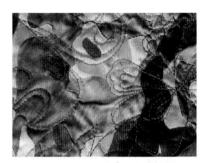

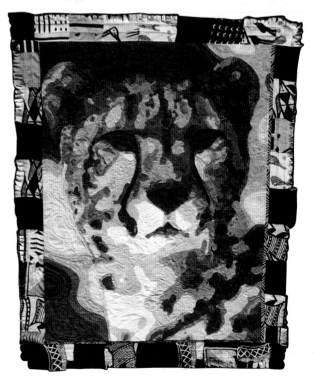

Stacy Hurt

Don't Say Goodbye | 2007

59 X 45 INCHES (149.9 X 114.3 CM)

Cotton batik, mud cloth, cotton batiste, fabrics, variegated thread; fused, machine quilted

PHOTOS BY ARTIST

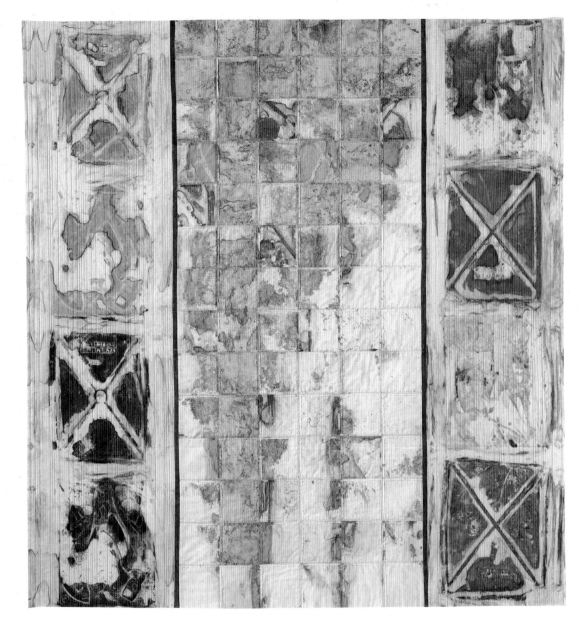

Charlotte Yde

Imprints of Time 4 | 2005

60 X 55 INCHES (152.4 X 139.7 CM)

Cotton; machine pieced, machine quilted

PHOTO BY ARTIST

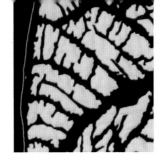

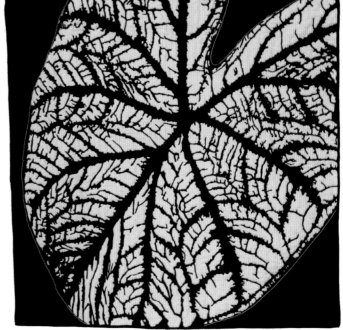

Wendy L. Starn

Shady Lady | 2008

26³/₄ X 27¹/₄ INCHES (67.9 X 69.2 CM)

Cotton; fused, machine appliquéd, quilted

PHOTOS BY ARTIST

Lisa M. Corson

Fossils IV | 2008

EACH PANEL 27 X 12 INCHES (68.6 X 30.5 CM)

Cotton; hand dyed, screen-printed, discharged, rusted, machine quilted, hand stitched

PHOTO BY ARTIST

Marjorie Post
Bandolier | 2007
46 X 33 INCHES (116.8 X 83.8 CM)
Cotton; hand dyed, raw-edge
appliquéd, machine stitched,
machine quilted
PHOTO BY BILL BACHHUBER

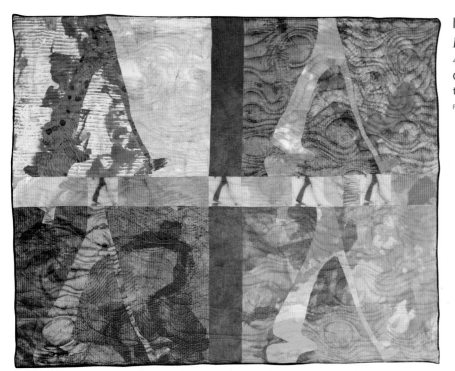

Moya Jones

Fountain Square | 2004

48 X 62 INCHES (121.9 X 157.5 CM)

Cotton, print; hand dyed, transferred, pieced

PHOTO BY CINDY WAGNER

Mary Tabar

Sea of Flowers | 2008

35 X 47 INCHES (88.9 X 119.4 CM)

Satin, photographs; printed, machine pieced, machine quilted

PHOTO BY RYAN PENNELL

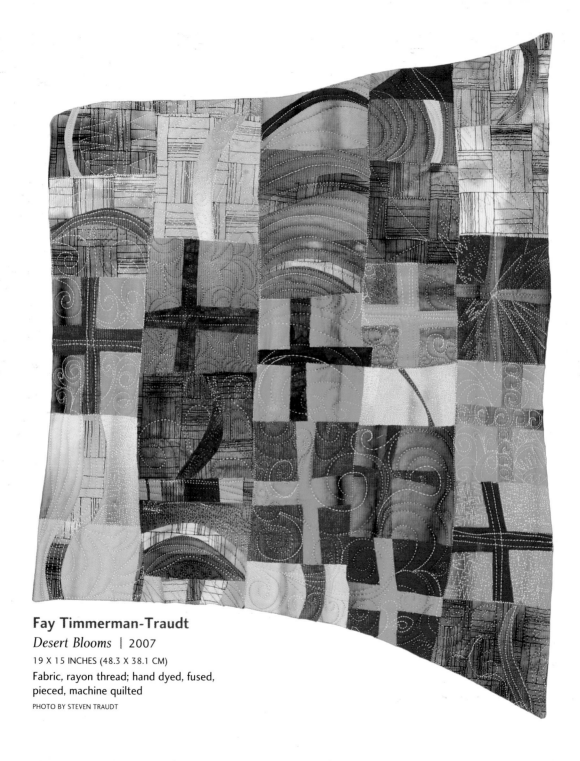

Fay Timmerman-Traudt

Desert Blooms | 2007

19 X 15 INCHES (48.3 X 38.1 CM)

Fabric, rayon thread; hand dyed, fused,
pieced, machine quilted

PHOTO BY STEVEN TRAUDT

Janet Twinn

Lightwave Variation | 2008

48 X 53 INCHES (121.9 X 134.6 CM)

Cotton, dye; painted, machine pieced, machine quilted

PHOTO BY ARTIST

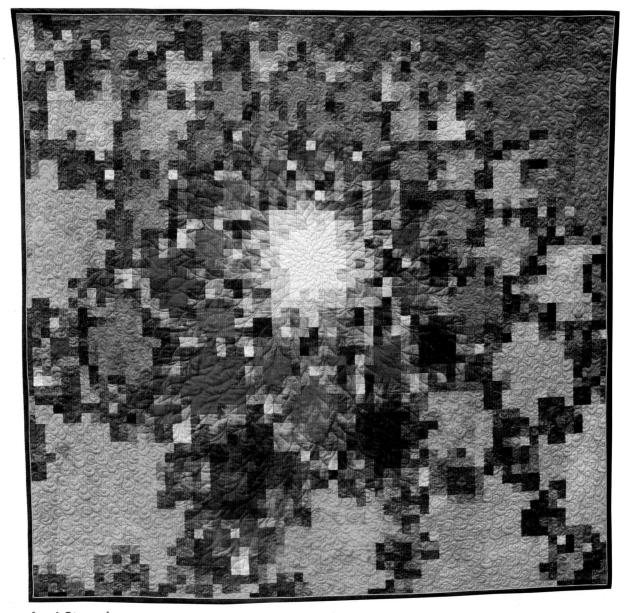

Jerri Stroud

Dahlia My Dreams | 2004

62¹/₂ X 60 INCHES (158.8 X 152.4 CM)

Cotton, variegated thread; hand dyed, machine pieced, machine quilted

PHOTO BY ARTIST

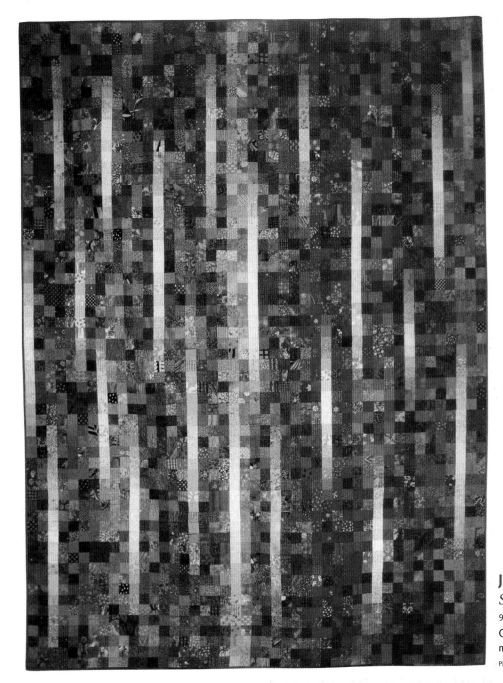

Jan Elliott
Shot in the Dark | 2008
91 X 68 INCHES (231.1 X 172.7 CM)
Cotton; machine pieced,
machine quilted
PHOTO BY ARTIST

Ineke van Unen

Evolution | 2006

48 X 48 INCHES (121.9 X 121.9 CM)

Commercial fabric, cotton, silk, velvet, plastic, linen, polyester, water-soluble
fleece; hand dyed, machine appliquéd, machine quilted, machine embroidered

PHOTO BY F.R. VAN UNEN

Jan Hutchison
It's Turtles All the Way Down | 2006
77 X 80 INCHES (195.6 X 203.2 CM)
Cotton, metallic thread, rayon thread; machine appliquéd, machine quilted
PHOTOS BY PETER HUTCHISON

Maureen O'Doogan
Surrender | 2008
45 X 35 INCHES (114.3 X 88.9 CM)
Cotton, cheesecloth, water-soluble stabilizer, yarn, wool roving; needle felted, fused, free-motion quilted
PHOTO BY ARTIST

Jane Kimball   **Dory Gossman**
Tippie Deleo   **Carol Korman**
Jane Fahey   **Penelope E. Mace**
Shirley Gallo   **Elizabeth Schamber**

Renoir Reassembled | 2005

59 X 70 INCHES (149.9 X 177.8 CM)

Cotton, silk, satin, beads; appliquéd, painted

PHOTO BY JANE KIMBALL

Karin Lusnak

Red Sky Rondelet | 2006

48 X 44 INCHES (121.9 X 111.8 CM)

Cotton; hand pieced, machine pieced, hand quilted

PHOTO BY SIBILA SAVAGE

Denise A. Currier
Mayo Clinic Celebrates
20 Years of Caring in Arizona,
Panel 1 of 3 | 2007

58 X 35 INCHES (147.3 X 88.9 CM)

Pima cotton, silks, batiks, sateen cotton, glass beads, copper, photographic images; hand dyed, discharged, painted, printed, enameled, machine pieced, machine quilted, machine appliquéd, hand embroidered

PHOTOS BY ARTIST AND DAVID R. CURRIER

Sue Holdaway-Heys

Tuscan Hideaway | 2007

44 X 68 INCHES (111.8 X 172.7 CM)

Cotton, commercial fabric; hand dyed,
fused, machine quilted, hand painted

Maureen O'Doogan

Me and the Pelican | 2008

48 X 48 INCHES (121.9 X 121.9 CM)

Cotton; needle felted, fused, raw-edge appliquéd, free-motion quilted

PHOTOS BY ARTIST

Catherine Nicholls

Sedna | 2006

70 X 30½ INCHES (177.8 X 77.5 CM)

Cotton, buttons, pen, ink; hand dyed, hand appliquéd, machine appliquéd, machine quilted, hand stitched

PHOTO BY ARTIST

Elizabeth Schamber

Patience: Waiting for the Wind | 2007

22 X 17 INCHES (55.9 X 43.2 CM)

Cotton fabric, rayon thread, metallic thread; machine appliquéd, thread embroidered

PHOTO BY ARTIST

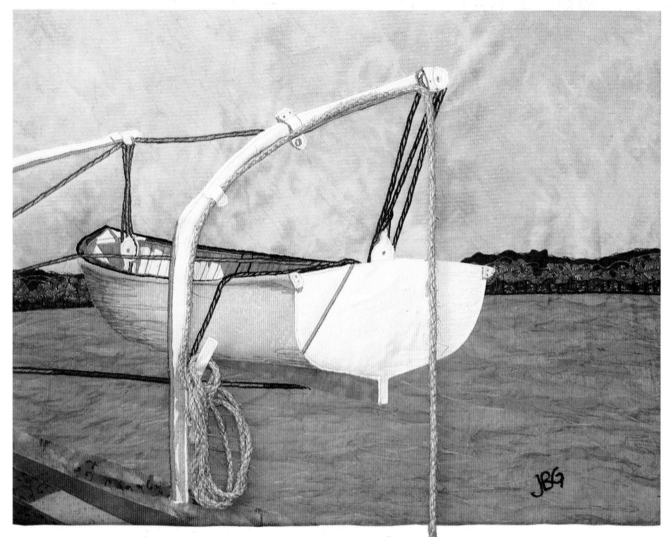

Jayne Bentley Gaskins

Peaceful Waters | 2008

22¹/₂ X 28 INCHES (57.2 X 71.1 CM)

Cotton, semi-transparent material, hemp rope;
machine appliquéd, machine quilted, fused

PHOTO BY ARTIST

Deborah K. Snider

Encrustaceans I | 2008

40 X 40 INCHES (101.6 X 101.6 CM)

Cotton, Swarovski crystals; raw-edge appliquéd, free-motion machine quilted

PHOTOS BY HAROLD D. SNIDER

Carol Anne Grotrian

Nobody Home | 2008

19 X 28 INCHES (45.7 X 71.1 CM)

Cotton, silk, fiber-reactive dyes, indigo; hand dyed, shibori, raw-edge appliquéd, hand appliquéd, hand quilted

PHOTO BY ARTIST

Ulla Andreasson

A Bright Summer Day | 2007

42 X 50 INCHES (106.6 X 127 CM)

Silk; machine quilted, machine appliquéd

PHOTO BY ARTIST

Terry Kramzar

Save Me from the Trilliums | 2005

54 X 70 INCHES (137.2 X 177.8 CM)

Cotton; hand dyed, hand appliquéd, machine appliquéd,
fused, machine quilted, thread embellished

PHOTO BY ARTIST

Virginia MacVeigh Cook

Seneca Schoolhouse, c. 1865, Poolesville, MD | 2008

14¹⁄₂ X 20 INCHES (36.8 X 50.8 CM)

Cotton, glue, polyester fiberfill; machine quilted

PHOTO BY LILIANE BLOM

Leslie Gabriëlse

Nature Vivante | 2008

60 X 86 INCHES (152.4 X 218.4 CM)

Fabric, yarn, pearl cotton thread, acrylic paints;
hand painted, hand sewn

PHOTOS BY ARTIST

Mary Tabar

Yesterday | 2008

54 X 52 INCHES (137.2 X 132.1 CM)

Cotton lawn, freezer paper, photographs;
printed, machine pieced, machine quilted

PHOTO BY RYAN PENNELL

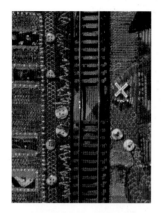

Pat Hardie

From Town to Country | 2008

17 X 34 INCHES (43.2 X 86.4 CM)

Upholstery fabrics, silk, wool, zippers,
HO-gauge railroad track, earrings, buttons;
hand appliquéd, machine quilted, embellished

PHOTOS BY ARTIST

Nancy G. Cook
Summer Split | 2008
36 X 28 INCHES (91.4 X 71.1 CM)
Cotton sateen, cotton gauze;
machine appliquéd,
machine quilted, inked,
hand embroidered
PHOTOS BY MITCHELL KEARNEY

Terri Stegmiller

Blue-mers Paper Quilt | 2008

11½ X 20½ INCHES (29.2 X 52.1 CM)

Cotton, interfacing, thread, newspaper, book pages,
tissue paper, textile paint, glue, acrylic paint, ink,
charcoal; collaged, glued, free-motion stitched

PHOTO BY ARTIST

Judy B. Dales

Floral Form II | 2006

39 X 30 INCHES (99 X 76.2 CM)

Cotton; machine pieced, machine quilted

PHOTO BY KAREN BELL

Kathy York

Vertigo | 2007

60 X 27½ INCHES (152.4 X 69.9 CM)

Cotton, plastic, embroidery floss, beads, copper wire; hand dyed, screen-printed, machine pieced, appliquéd, hand beaded, hand embroidered, embellished, machine quilted, painted

PHOTO BY ARTIST

Linda Lunt

Long Life with Happiness | 2002

34½ X 28 INCHES (87.6 X 71.1 CM)

Cotton, organza, gold metallic thread;
raw-edge machine appliquéd,
hand quilted

PHOTOS BY MARK FREY

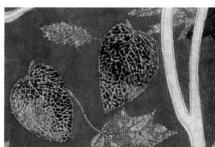

Vivien Zepf

Revelation | 2007

24 X 23 INCHES (61.0 X 58.4 CM)

Cotton, batiks, fabric paint; hand
dyed, raw-edge appliquéd, free-motion
machine quilted, trapunto

PHOTO BY ARTIST

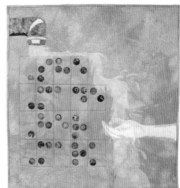

Andrea L. Stern

Bird's-Eye View | 2006

24 X 18 INCHES (61.0 X 45.7 CM)

Cotton, silk, beads, sequins, fusible appliqué;
machine pieced, machine quilted

PHOTO BY MARTY STERN

Debra Daw Lamm
Interference #3 | 2007
22 X 17 INCHES (55.9 X 43.2 CM)

Cotton, nylon organza, paper; printed, painted, layered, machine quilted

PHOTO BY JOSEPH D. LAMM

Heather Allen-Swarttouw

Arboretum #8 | 2001

23 X 36 INCHES (58.4 X 91.4 CM)

Cotton, linen, silk, dye, textile inks, paste
resist, dye; machine quilted

PHOTO BY TIM BARNWELL

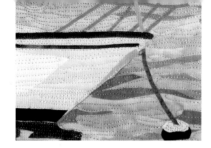

Melinda Bula

Monterey at Dusk | 2007

51 X 60 INCHES (129.5 X 152.4 CM)

Cotton, rayon thread, fusible appliqué; machine quilted

PHOTOS BY ARTIST

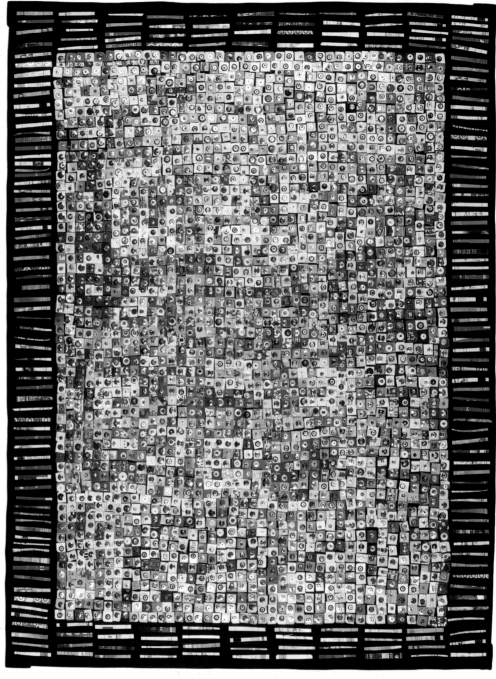

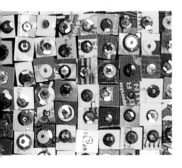

Amy Orr
Credit Card Quilt:
Security Measures | 2006
39 X 30 INCHES (99.1 X 76.2 CM)
Plastic cards, velvet;
cut, drilled, beaded
PHOTOS BY JOHN WOODIN

Mary S. Buvia

String of Pearls | 2007

84 X 75 INCHES (213.4 X 190.5 CM)

Cotton, iridescent film, crystals; machine appliquéd, double-thread appliquéd, couched, piped, free-motion embroidered, machine quilted

PHOTOS BY ROBERT D. BUVIAV

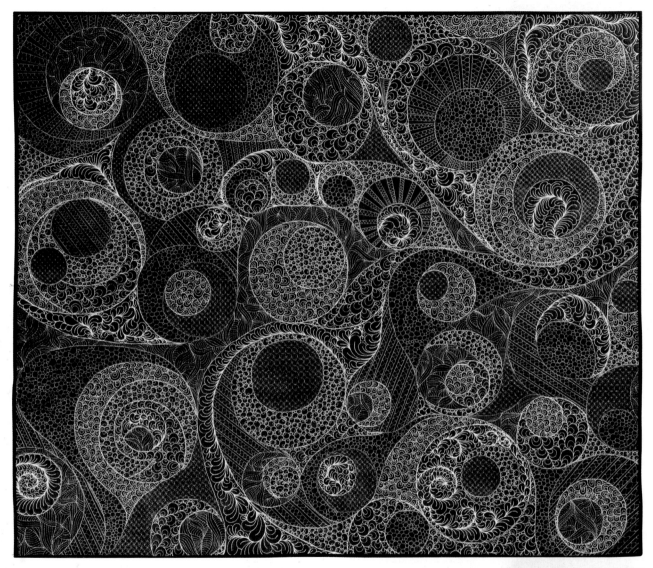

Maria G. Shell
A. Hofmann's Obit | 2008
52 X 62 INCHES (132.1 X 157.5 CM)
Whole cloth, thread; long-arm quilted
PHOTOS BY CHRIS AREND

Virginia A. Spiegel

Boundary Waters 21 | 2007

24½ X 34 INCHES (62.2 X 86.4 CM)

Cotton, duck cloth, acrylic paint, silk organza,
oil paintstick, thread; inkjet printed, screen-printed,
lettered, stitched

PHOTOS BY JOSEPH T. EDOM

Dena Dale Crain

Spirit Works: Heart's Aflutter | 2006

24 X 28 INCHES (61.0 X 71.1 CM)

Cotton, acrylic fabric paint, sequins; machine quilted,
hand painted, hand beaded

PHOTO BY ARTIST

Annette Morgan
Silver Triangles | 2004
36 X 24 INCHES (91.4 X 61.0 CM)
Paper, plastic, polyester,
soldering iron, heat gun;
cut, stitched

PHOTO BY KEVIN MEAD

419

Jane Hall

Hope Is That Thing with Feathers | 2003

52 X 52 INCHES (132.1 X 132.1 CM)

Cotton, feathers; machine pieced,
machine quilted, hand quilted

PHOTO BY ARTIST

Lisa M. Penny

Garden of Daedalus | 2008

72 X 72 INCHES (182.9 X 182.9 CM)

Cotton, silk yarn, cashmere yarn, polyester
yarn, beads, silk flowers, satin flowers;
machine pieced, appliquéd, free-motion
machine quilted, hand stitched

PHOTOS BY ARTIST

Maya Schonenberger

Yangtze 1 | 2008

20 X 20 INCHES (50.8 X 50.8 CM)

Cotton, paper, printed material; painted, machine stitched, glued

PHOTO BY WERNER BOEGLIN

Betty Busby

Silverlight | 2008

78 X 90 INCHES (198.1 X 228.6 CM)

Cotton sateen, metallic thread, paint sticks; hand dyed, discharged, stenciled, raw-edge machine appliquéd, surface decorated

PHOTO BY ALAN MITCHELL PHOTOGRAPHY

Heidi Field-Alvarez
Smoke; Ode to Fragonard | 2008
36 X 28 INCHES (91.4 X 71.1 CM)
Canvas, satin, lace, acrylic paint;
machine quilted, free-motion quilted
PHOTO BY ARTIST

Jenny Williams

North Carolina Forests—Under Fire II | 2008

22 X 17 INCHES (55.9 X 43.2 CM)

Cotton; hand painted, machine appliquéd,
free-motion thread painted

Susan V. Polansky

Pastoral Disturbance | 2008

44 X 52 INCHES (111.8 X 132.1 CM)

Cotton, tulle, thread, fusible web, cotton/polyester batting;
collaged, machine quilted

Barbara Barrick McKie

My New Buddy | 2008

23¼ X 31¼ INCHES (59.1 X 79.4 CM)

Polyester crepe, wool batting, cotton backing; disperse dyed, trapunto, machine embroidered, machine appliquéd, machine quilted

PHOTOS BY ARTIST

Pat Kumicich

We're All the Same—Just Different | 2006

51 X 54 INCHES (129.5 X 137.2 CM)

Cotton, paint; machine pieced, hand stitched

PHOTO BY ARTIST

About the Juror

Karey Patterson Bresenhan is the president of Quilts, Inc., and the director of the International Quilt Festival, the United States' largest quilt event. She serves as the director of the International Quilt Market, the world's only wholesale tradeshow for the quilting industry. From 1974 to 2003, Bresenhan ran the Great Expectations Quilt Shop in Houston, Texas, one of the largest quilt stores in the United States. A fifth-generation Texas quilter, she is a member of the Quilters Hall of Fame and serves on the national board of Studio Art Quilt Associates (SAQA), the nation's leading organization of art quilters. She has written nine quilt reference books.

Bresenhan holds a bachelor of science degree from Sam Houston State University and a master's degree in journalism from the University of Texas. In 2008, she was elected mayor of the City of Piney Point Village, a community near Houston, Texas, where she has lived with her husband since 1988.

Acknowledgments

This beautiful book is a credit both to a wide array of talented professionals and a diverse, growing craft category that only recently has begun receiving its proper due in the art world. Juror Karey Patterson Bresenhan is a passionate advocate for the entire quilt community—which encompasses both traditional quilts and art quilts—and she juried the book's selections with discernment, wisdom, and great care. Karey also was simply a delight to work with. Martha Sielman, executive director of Studio Art Quilt Associates (SAQA) and curator of *Masters: Art Quilts* and *Masters: Art Quilts, Volume 2*, provided generous assistance and support—as well as encouragement—throughout the book's development.

At Lark Books, the terrific editorial trio of Julie Hale, Dawn Dillingham, and Susan Kieffer facilitated a seamless publishing process. The art design and production team of Kay Stafford, Kathy Holmes, Carol Morse, and Shannon Yokeley was equally outstanding. Fitting 500 quilts in an 8-inch-square book is a fine challenge, and I'm so impressed and grateful that this group was able to present all the wonderful work in such spectacular ways.

Most of all, of course, my thanks go out to each of the quilt artists whose head, heart, and hands gave birth to the collection of extraordinary art quilts we feature in these pages. Thank you for sharing your creative visions.

Ray Hemachandra
Senior Editor

Contributing Artists

Adams, Christine L.
Rockville, Maryland
30

Adams, Deidre
Littleton, Colorado
355

Adler, Fran Cowen
Manchester, Michigan
128

Allen, Pamela
Kingston, Ontario, Canada
361

Allen, Renée M.
Atlanta, Georgia
170

Allen-Swarttouw, Heather
Asheville, North Carolina
412

Andreasson, Ulla
Maerne di Martellago, Italy
400

Ansbaugh, Colleen
Manitowoc, Wisconsin
182, 341

Aristova, Ludmila
Brooklyn, New York
247, 342

Arnold, Mary
Vancouver, Washington
54

Austin, Esterita
Port Jefferson Station, New York
344

Baker, Rosalie
Davenport, Iowa
94, 219

Barkley, Teresa
Maplewood, New Jersey
36

Barlow, Linda
Shropshire, England
109, 267, 354

Barton, Elizabeth
Athens, Georgia
156, 191, 245

Beasley, Alice
Oakland, California
281, 371

Belford, Marilyn
Chenango Forks, New York
67, 81

Benson, Regina V.
Golden, Colorado
207

Berns, Wendy Butler
Lake Mills, Wisconsin
116, 332

Billingslea, Alessandra
Post Falls, Idaho
31, 350

Binkley, Lisa
Waunakee, Wisconsin
44

Bird, Charlotte
San Diego, California
141

Bornemisza, Eszter
Budapest, Hungary
339

Bowers, Mary Jo
Chicago, Illinois
58, 159

Bowser, Tammie
South Pasadena, California
99, 224

Bracy, Diana
Las Vegas, Nevada
120

Brainerd, Laurie
San Antonio, Texas
298

Breckner, Sharon
Hastings Nebraska
57

Brokenshire, Andrea M.
Round Rock, Texas
66

Brown, Christina
Portland, Oregon
320

Brown, Nancy S.
Oakland, California
238, 328, 329

Brucar, Shelley
Buffalo Grove, Illinois
77

Bula, Melinda
El Dorado Hills, California
129, 131, 413

Burr, Marianne
Coupeville, Washington
47

Busby, Betty
Albuquerque, New Mexico
253, 422

Buvia, Mary S.
Greenwood, Indiana
415

Carabas, Leslie C.
Sonora, California
256

Carlstrom, Lucinda
Atlanta, Georgia
211

Cashatt Deb
Cameron Park, California
315

Cassidy, Carol
Charlottesville, Virginia
307

Catlin, Cynthia H.
San Pedro, California
63

Cavazos, Violet O.
Falls Church, Virginia
206

Cherian, Leela
Bangalore, Karnataka, India
131

Cherry, Donna
Bend, Oregon
144, 168

Chin, Shin-hee
McPherson, Kansas
361

Clawson, Susanne
Silver Spring, Maryland
237

Cochran, Jane Burch
Rabbit Hash, Kentucky
197, 200

Coleman, Marion
Castro Valley, California
201

Connor, Kathleen W.
Chesapeake Beach, Maryland
145

Content, Judith
Palo Alto, California
175

Cook, Nancy G.
Charlotte, North Carolina
325, 406

Cook, Virginia MacVeigh
Darnestown, Maryland
409

Cooper, Janet
Sheffield, Massachusetts
177

Corson, Lisa M.
Bristol, Connecticut
383

Crain, Dena Dale
Nakura, Kenya
418

Crasco, Nancy
Brighton, Massachusetts
320

Crawford, Lenore
Midland, Michigan
26, 171, 189

Cullen, Phyllis
Chico, California
97

Currier, Denise A.
Mesa, Arizona
394

Dales, Judy B.
Greensboro, Vermont
408

Deleo, Tippie
Reedville, Virginia
392

Deuel, Joan Lockburner
Richford, New York
110

Diamond, Mary
Sheldrake, New York
127

Dickey, Nancy B.
Magnolia, Texas
336

Dillon, Sally
Amherst, Massachusetts
48, 76

Dolan, Pat
State College, Pennsylvania
208

Dosho, Chiaki
Kawasaki-shi, Kanagawa-ken, Japan
116

Doughty, Eileen
Vienna, Virginia
243, 246

Douglas, Avril
Alston, Cumbria, England
34

Drucker, Tamar
Ossining, New York
225

Drummond, Carol
Gainesville, Florida
41

Dunnewold, Jane
San Antonio, Texas
140

Duschack, Julie
Denmark, Wisconsin
380

Eckley, Ginny
Kingwood, Texas
79, 316, 324

Eddy, Ellen Anne
Porter, Indiana
242

Einstein, Sylvia H.
Belmont, Massachusetts
204

Elking, Leigh
Scottsdale, Arizona
147

Elliott, Jan
Nassau, Bahamas
389

Elmusa, Mary
Leawood, Kansas
319

Endo, Noriko
Narashino, Chiba, Japan
241, 321

Errea, Grace J.
Laguna Niguel, California
180

Evans, Diane J.
Schenectady, New York
230

Fahey, Jane
Reedville, Virginia
392

Fahl, Ann
Racine, Wisconsin
223

Fallert, Caryl Bryer
Paducah, Kentucky
295, 333

Farquhar, Marilyn
Kitchener, Ontario, Canada
115

Faulkner, Patricia G.
Rochester, New York
255

Fay, Liz Alpert
Sandy Hook, Connecticut
32

Fell, Deborah
Urbana, Illinois
91

Ferrono, Clairan
Chicago, Illinois
338

Fiddes, Margo
Edmonton, Alberta, Canada
372, 375

Field-Alvarez, Heidi
Richmond, Virginia
123, 423

Fingal, Jamie
Orange, California
161

Firth, Dianne
Canberra, Australia
273

Fisher, Deborah
Stony Brook, New York
113

Fitterman, Mindy
Concord, New Hampshire
363

Fitzsimmons, Tommy
Romeoville, Illinois
327

Flamme, Karen
Oakland, California
256, 287

Flynn, Candy
Middleton, Wisconsin
305

Fogg, Laura
Ukiah, California
181, 359

Frankel, Melissa K.
Mashpee, Massachusetts
148, 229

Frizzell, Linda Rudin
Rural Mason County, Washington
284

Fromherz, Marilyn
Calimesa, California
143

Gabel, Debra
Clarksville, Maryland
268

Gabriëlse, Leslie
Rotterdam, Netherlands
403

Gallo, Shirley
Reedville, Virginia
392

Gant, Alice Leck
Trumansburg, New York
180

Gardner, Bodil
Lystrup, Denmark
266, 269

Garrard, Alice Fuchs
West Redding, Connecticut
146

Garstecki, Darlene
Hot Springs Village, Arkansas
142

Gaskins, Jayne Bentley
Fernandina Beach, Florida
349, 398

Gass, Linda
Los Altos, California
14, 271

Gilbert, Beth P.
Buffalo Grove, Illinois
318

Goetzinger, Karen
Ottawa, Ontario, Canada
133, 139

Golenia, Jo-Ann
Venice, Florida
183, 261

Goodall, Margery
Mount Lawley, Australia
362

Gooding, Hilary
Corfe Mullen, Dorset, England
356

Goodson, Mary
Silverton, Oregon
240

Goodwin, Valerie S.
Tallahassee, Florida
13

Gossman, Dory
Reedville, Virginia
392

Gould, Patricia
Albuquerque, New Mexico
82

Gregg, Sandy
Cambridge, Massachusetts
356

Gregory, Deborah K.
Bellevue, Washington
179

Grotrian, Carol Anne
Cambridge, Massachusetts
399

Habicht, Desiree Dianne
Riverside, California
51, 145

Hall, Leslie A.
Longboat Key, Florida
327

Hall, Linda
Douglassville, Pennsylvania
290

Haller, Robin M.
Carbondale, Illinois
352

Hamilton-McNally, Molly Y.
Tehachapi, California
234

Hansen, Gloria
East Windsor, New Jersey
100, 330

Hardie, Pat
Merrickville, Ontario, Canada
405

Hartman, Barbara Oliver
Flower Mound, Texas
184, 294

Harwell, Ann
Wendell, North Carolina
12, 205

Hattabaugh, Marla
Scottsdale, Arizona
364

Havlan, Denise Tallon
Plainfield, Illinois
108, 195

Hearder, Valerie
Mahone Bay, Nova Scotia, Canada
291

Hearn, Jenny
Johannesburg, South Africa
232

Hendricks, Annette M.
Grayslake, Illinois
194

Henrion, Marilyn
New York, New York
70

Hergert, Anna
Moose Jaw, Saskatchewan, Canada
357

Heus, Mary Ellen
Waukesha, Wisconsin
111

Hoefner, Sandra
Grand Junction, Colorado
124, 369

Holdaway-Heys, Sue
Ann Arbor, Michigan
303, 347, 395

Horansky, Ruby
Brooklyn, New York
70

Hueber, Inge
Cologne, Germany
103

Hughes, Rose
Signal Hill, California
259

Hurt, Stacy
Orange, California
381

Hutchison, Jan
Sedgwick, Kansas
391

Iida, Harumi
Kamakura, Japan
117

Jensen, Jill
Lynchburg, Virginia
216, 296, 312,

Jensen, Marie
Tacoma, Washington
367

Johnson, Beth Porter
Houston, Texas
274, 373

Jones, Jessica Elizabeth
Smithville, Tennessee
208

Jones, Moya
Fairfield, Ohio
385

Judd, Jean M.
Cushing, Wisconsin
262

Kagerer, Margit
Carefree, Arizona
152

Kaplan, Anita
The Sea Ranch, California
244, 323

Keister, Ann Baddeley
Grand Rapids, Michigan
38

Kempers-Cullen, Natasha
Topsham, Maine
43, 370

Kersey, Toni
Philadelphia, Pennsylvania
381

Kim, Misik
Seoul, South Korea
19

Kimball, Jane
Reedville, Virginia
392

Kleeman, Catherine
Baltimore, Maryland
340

Kluepfel, Marjan
Davis, California
86, 132

Knott, Holly
Finger Lakes Region, New York
59, 347

Kongs, Sue
Cripple Creek, Colorado
213

Korman, Carol
Reedville, Virginia
392

Kowaleski, Ann
Mount Pleasant, Michigan
40

Kramzar, Terry
Kennett Square, Pennsylvania
33, 401

Kreneck, Ellie
Lubbock, Texas
135

Kroth, Pat
Verona, Wisconsin
250

Krueger, Susan
Bowling Green, Ohio
314

Kumicich, Pat
Naples, Florida
5, 10, 427

Kurjan, Janet
Lake Forest Park, Washington
174

Lacy, Marguerite J.
Auburn, California
53

Lamm, Debra Daw
Spokane, Washington
411

Lampi-Legaree, Shawna
Yellowknife, Northwest Territories, Canada
49

Lanaux, Juanita
Columbus, Georgia
227

Lange, Barbara
Freising, Germany
137

Lasher, Gay E.
Denver, Colorado
221

Lawrence, Clara
Elgin, Texas
169

Lee, Kathy Angel
Old Orchard Beach, Maine
83

Levin, Linda
Wayland, Massachusetts
190, 237

Levin, Linda
Wayland, Massachusetts
190, 237

Lichtendahl, Kathy
Clark, Wyoming
107

Lindner, Ellen
Melbourne, Florida
22, 98, 295

Lockhart, Cynthia
Cincinnati, Ohio
62, 172

Londir, Aryana B.
New River, Arizona
212

Lovett, Vita Marie
Maryville, Tennessee
29

Lovinger, Margot
Seattle, Washington
122, 277

Lullie, Anne
Lake in the Hills, Illinois
72, 175

Lumsden, Susan Leslie
Thayer, Missouri
149

Lunt, Linda
Bothell, Washington
409

Lusnak, Karin
Albany, California
393

Mace, Penelope E.
Reedville, Virginia
93, 392

MacGregor, Shirley H.
Portland, Oregon
74

Maley, Ann Miller
Martha's Vineyard, Massachusetts
130

Martin, Karen Colbourne
St. John's, Newfoundland, Canada
140, 192

Mazuran, Cody Marie
Salt Lake City, Utah
285

McCabe, Kathleen
Coronado, California
280

McCain, Eleanor A.
Shalimur, Florida
199

McHale, Teri
Oceanside, California
277

McKie, Barbara Barrick
Lyme, Connecticut
83, 426

McNeil, Kathy
Tulalip Washington
95, 115, 292, 309

Meyer, Jeannette DeNicolis
Portland, Oregon
102

Mijanovich, Jim
Marshall, North Carolina
125

Mijanovich, Libby
Marshall, North Carolina
125

Miller, Beth
Kambah, Australia
365

Miller, Denise Oyama
Fremont, California
98

Moore, Dottie
Rock Hill, South Carolina
84

Moore, Jeannie Palmer
Escondido, California
363

Morgan, Annette
Bury St Edmunds, Suffolk, England
358, 419

Morgenthaler, Luella
Boulder, Colorado
228

Morin, Lynne
Kanata, Ontario, Canada
24

Morrissey, Carol
Double Oaks, Texas
65, 346

Muir, Alison
Neutral Bay, New South Wales, Australia
151, 155, 186

Murkin, Scott A.
Asheboro, North Carolina
75

Murty, Nancy
Farmington, New York
351, 378

Myers-Newbury, Jan
Pittsburgh, Pennsylvania
306

Nancarrow, Ree
Denali Park, Alaska
302

Nash, Dominie
Bethesda, Maryland
104

Naylor, Philippa
Beverley, East Yorkshire, England
60

Naylor, Sylvia
Cambridge, Ontario, Canada
254

Neblett, Jean
San Francisco, California
214

Nicholls, Catherine
West Vancouver, British Columbia, Canada
397

Nickolson, Anne McKenzie
Indianapolis, Indiana
264, 296

Nida, Kathy
El Cajon, California
217

Nordlin, Stephanie
Poplar Grove, Illinois
270, 301

Norton, Constance
Fairfax, Virginia
167

O'Doogan, Maureen
Tallahassee, Florida
391, 396

Olfe, Dan
Julian, California
331

Olson, Barbara
Billings, Montana
112, 230

Orr, Amy
Philadelphia, Pennsylvania
414

Otto, Barbara
Stillwater, Minnesota
136

Ouellette, Bonnie B.
Seneca, South Carolina
265

Owoc, Pat
St. Louis, Missouri
353

Pagliai, Shelly
Macon, Missouri
73

Paquin, Gabrielle
Orleans, France
164

Parillo, Marlene Ferrell
Lincolndale, New York
319

Parker, Anne R.
Hoi An, Vietnam
330

Parson, Emily
Saint Charles, Illinois
50

Pelish, Lori Lupe
Niskayuna, New York
126, 377

Penny, Lisa M.
Ridgefield, Connecticut
420

Pepe, MaryLou
Boalsburg, Pennsylvania
101, 160

Perez, Judy Coates
Chicago, Illinois
18

Pfaff, Julia E.
Richmond, Virginia
162, 326

Phillips, Margaret A.
Cos Cob, Connecticut
168

Pignatelli, Vikki
Reynoldsburg, Ohio
342, 348

Polansky, Susan V.
Boston, Massachusetts
24, 425

Pollock, Michele Heather
Columbus, Indiana
238

Polston, Barbara
Phoenix, Arizona
239

Poole, Elizabeth
Garrison, New York
360

Porcella, Yvonne
Modesto, California
61, 339

Post, Marjorie
Portland, Oregon
384

Powers, Ruth
Carbondale, Kansas
231, 335

Puetz, Casey
Waukesha, Wisconsin
118

Quehl, Elaine
Ottawa, Ontario, Canada
297, 348, 370

Quinlan, Shawn
Pittsburgh, Pennsylvania
42

Randol, Melody
Loveland, Colorado
251, 293, 364

Redmond, Wen
Strafford, New Hampshire
251

Reed, B.J.
St. Thomas, Pennsylvania
286

Reed, Suanne
Chicago, Illinois
372

Rego, Leslie
Sun Valley, Idaho
166, 233

Remick, Helen
Seattle, Washington
163

Rickman, Jan
Whitewater, Colorado
56

Rienzo, Susan
Vero Beach, Florida
262

Riggio, Suzanne Mouton
Wauwatosa, Wisconsin
134

Rimkus-Falconer, Shirley Jo
Independence, Oregon
52

Ritter, Kim
Houston, Texas
283

Rocke, Lora
Lincoln, Nebraska
21

Rossi, Lonni
Wynnewood, Pennsylvania
179, 211

Rother, Carmella Karijo
Ottawa, Ontario, Canada
209

Rowell, Bernie
Candler North Carolina
45

Ruthsdottir, Ann E.
Brunswick, Maine
226

Salzman, Pauline
Treasure Island, Florida
196

Sassaman, Jane
Harvard, Illinois
71

Savona, Diane
Passaic, New Jersey
203

Sazaki, Kris
Cameron Park, California
315

Schamber, Elizabeth
Wicomico Church, Virginia
392, 397

Schlueter, Julie A.
Orange, California
47

Schneider, Barbara J.
Woodstock, Illinois
154

Schonenberger, Maya
Miami, Florida
222, 421

Schulze, Joan
Sunnyvale, California
176

Schwalb, Robin
Brooklyn, New York
35, 105

Sellers, Sally A.
Vancouver, Washington
202

Shapel, Barbara
Washougal, Washington
114

Sharkey, Diana F.
Mount Kisco, New York
311

Shaw, Patti
Seattle, Washington
272, 368

Shelenberger, Sandy
Conneaut, Ohio
273

Shell, Maria G.
Anchorage, Alaska
416

Sherman, Mark
Coral Springs, Florida
119

Shevell, Judith
Bridgewater, New Jersey
232

Shie, Susan
Wooster, Ohio
235, 275

Shine, Sherry D.
East Orange, New Jersey
20, 134, 341

Shippy, Teresa
Santa Ana, California
80

Simpson, Valentyna Roenko
Oceanside, California
158

Smith, Bonnie J.
San Jose, California
120

Smith, Brenda Gael
Copacabana, New South Wales, Australia
151

Smith, Brenda H.
Flagstaff, Arizona
96

Smith, Clare
Wellington, New Zealand
301

Smith, Diane W.
Merritt Island, Florida
157, 215

Smith, Louisa L.
Loveland, Colorado
354

Smith, Mary Ruth
Waco, Texas
88, 203

Smith, Sarah Ann
Camden, Maine
76, 198

Snider, Deborah K.
Grand Junction, Colorado
109, 282, 399

Sorrell, Susan R.
Greenville, South Carolina
220

Sowada, Joan
Gillette, Wyoming
188, 279, 374

Spiegel, Virginia A.
Byron, Illinois
417

Starn, Wendy L.
Alexandria, Louisiana
383

Steadman, Janet
Langley, Washington
51

Stegmiller, Terri
Mandan, North Dakota
407

Stein, Marcia
San Francisco, California
28, 141

Steinhauer, Margarete
Scituate, Massachusetts
153

Stern, Andrea L.
Chauncey, Ohio
300, 410

Stewart, Andrea
Scituate, Massachusetts
249

Stroud, Jerri
Webster Groves, Missouri
388

Strumwasser, Wendy F.
Plainview, New York
165

Swearington, Jen
Asheville, North Carolina
11, 78, 304

Sweeney, Eileen Klee
Niles, Michigan
110

Sylvester, Deborah
Marysville, Washington
20, 68, 360

Symes, Sarah
San Rafael, California
343

Tabar, Mary
San Diego, California
385, 404

Taylor, Carol
Pittsford, New York
138, 366

Taylor, David
Steamboat Springs, Colorado
58, 178

Taylor, Rhoda E.
Slippery Rock, Pennsylvania
92

Thiele, Pamela
Lakewood, Colorado
46

Timmerman-Traudt, Fay
Grand Junction, Colorado
386

Tolksdorf, Odette
Durban, South Africa
313

Trefethen, Gwyned
Sherborn, Massachusetts
3, 90

Trusty, Ann
Lawrence, Kansas
55

Tweed, Kristin
Fort Myers, Florida
260, 278

Twinn, Janet
Tadworth, Surrey, England
387

Vahl, Meri Henriques
Soquel, California
106

van der Veen, Grietje
Oberwil, Switzerland
302

Van Horn, Larkin Jean
Whidbey Island, Washington
309

van Unen, Ineke
Heerguowaard, Netherlands
299, 390

van Velzen, Sandra
Tiel, Netherlands
248

von der Heiden, Beatrix
Leun, Germany
37

Vredenburg, Elsie
Tustin, Michigan
288

Wademan, Sue
Queenstown, New Zealand
187

Waldron, Terry
Anaheim, California
27, 322

Wall, Marilyn H.
West Union, South Carolina
23, 345

Warkentin, Nelda
Anchorage, Alaska
150, 236

Wasilowski, Laura
Elgin, Illinois
287

Watkins, Carol
Boulder, Colorado
16, 252, 309

Watler, Barbara W.
Hollywood, Florida
307, 317

Waugh, Carol Ann
Denver, Colorado
64, 87

Weir, Sylvia
Beaumont, Texas
121

Weiss, Maggie
Evanston, Illinois
258, 337

West, Barbara J.
Canmore, Alberta, Canada
193

Wheatley-Wolf, Jennifer A.
Arlington, Virginia
334

White, Ruth A.
Ithaca, New York
113

White, Valerie C.
Louisville, Kentucky
257

Willen, Susan K.
Redondo Beach, California
65

Williams, Jenny
Lexington, North Carolina
424

Williams, Kent
Madison, Wisconsin
210, 313

Williamson, Barbara
Paradise, California
227

Wilson, Lois Puckett
Lincoln, Nebraska
185

Wood, LM
Graham, North Carolina
48, 218

Woods, Elia
Oklahoma City, Oklahoma
376

Wyatt, Mary Ev
Kingston, Ontario, Canada
173

Yde, Charlotte
FRB C, Denmark
382

Yeager, Juanita G.
Columbia, Missouri
55, 297

York, Kathy
Austin, Texas
15, 408

Zave, Pamela
Chatham, New Jersey
310

Zepf, Vivien
Thornwood, New York
410

Ziebarth, Charlotte
Boulder, Colorado
89, 289

Ziv, Ita
Pardes-Hana, Israel
263